"After being raped in college, I believe that all work for the empowerment of women is important, essential. This Goddess series creates a movement towards this effort of **awakening women to their power** – power which is limitless, in truth. Ava Miles is a courageous fellow writer whose mission is to empower all women."
—Aspen Matis, author of the internationally bestselling memoir, *Girl in the Woods*

"Ava **gets to the heart** of why some of us do toxic or hang around drama while helping us all realize we can have happy and loving relationships that don›t clutter up our space or make us sick."
—Courtney Cachet, Celebrity Designer & TV Personality

PRAISE FOR *THE GODDESS GUIDES*

"The shaming we go through as women is incredible. We even shame each other. It's about time someone called it out and gave us the tools to reclaim our everyday joy and honest expression. *The Goddess Guides* are a **world changer**. Well done, Ava."
—International Bestseller Kate Perry aka Kathia Zolfaghari, Artist & Activist

"Emboldened, shocking and necessary, *The Goddess Guides to Being a Woman* is a **life-changing journey** every woman will want to take."
—Crystal Andrus Morissette, Founder of the S.W.A.T. Institute (Simply Woman Accredited Trainer)

"Author Ava Miles redefines and alters the experience of shame for women and for the men who love them. Power comes from the way you speak and listen. Miles' series is an **exquisite exploration** of internal discomfort and courage, allowing you to reclaim your divine soul and fully express your womanhood. I highly recommend."
—Dr. Shawne Duperon, Project Forgive Founder, Nobel Peace Prize Nominee

"Miles provides us with **essential advice** on how we can shed the beliefs that are making us miserable and find our way back to our inner goddesses... She guides us through the sometimes turbulent waters of the issues that matter most to us (relationships, sex, finances, self-expression, self-image, etc.). **This is must reading for every goddess woman.**"
—Angela Polidoro, former Editor for Random House's Ballantine Bantam Dell

"Pushing the envelope is edgy. Change is never comfortable. Ava Miles takes us out of our comfortable chitchat cocoon and shows us how to become those butterflies all women are destined to become no matter what they face in life. The series is a **must-read.**"
—Risa Shimoda, Outdoor Leadership Consultant and President of The Shimoda Group

"This Goddess series unleashes the **inner power** we all have. Let your adventure begin and unleash by reading this series."
—Anna Levesque, author of *Yoga for Paddling*

"This series delivers **empowering advice** without pulling any punches."
—Liza M. Shaw, MA, Licensed Marriage and Family Therapist of PowerToThrive.com

Also by Ava Miles

The Goddess Guides to Being a Woman

Goddesses Decide
Goddesses Deserve The G's
Goddesses Love Cock
Goddesses Cry and Say Motherfucker
Goddesses Don't Do Drama
Goddesses Are Sexy
Goddesses Eat

Other Non-Fiction

The Happiness Corner: Reflections So Far

Fiction

The Dare Valley Series

Nora Roberts Land
French Roast
The Grand Opening
The Holiday Serenade
The Town Square
The Park of Sunset Dreams
The Perfect Ingredient
The Bridge to a Better Life

The Calendar of New Beginnings
Home Sweet Love
The Moonlight Serenade
Daring Brides

The Dare River Series

Country Heaven
Country Heaven Song Book
Country Heaven Cookbook
The Chocolate Garden
The Chocolate Garden:
A Magical Tale (Children's Book)
Fireflies and Magnolias
The Promise of Rainbows
The Fountain of Infinite Wishes

Dare Valley Meets Paris Billionaire Mini-Series

The Billionaire's Gamble
The Billionaire's Courtship
The Billionaire's Secret
The Billionaire's Return

goddesses
are sexy

Enjoying a
Loving Self-Image

Ava Miles

Legal Disclaimer

ISBN-10: 1-940565-72-3
ISBN-13: 978-1-940565-72-9
www.avamiles.com
Ava Miles

This one's going out to the two groups who've had the greatest influence on my journey in being a sexy goddess woman with swagger.

The women of Paris for showing me what it looks like to be sexy, unique, and connected—all so effortlessly—because it's how we're made.

Rap artists for sharing divine truths in rhyme and rhythm—either consciously or unconsciously; who knew my divine entourage would lead me there, but I am so glad they did.

Table of Contents

The Goddess Guides

Introduction

We're all goddesses and gods in a body.

The first time I heard this declaration, I knew on a soul level it was true. In my Catholic upbringing, I commonly heard I was a child of God. When I grew up, I wasn't a child anymore, but instead of being accepted as a goddess in a body, I was told I was human, and as such, imperfect.

The human part is right. The imperfect part is not.

If you're reading this, you've come awake to the truth like me. You've remembered you're a goddess or god in a body.

My goddess nature—my higher self or my soul—is the perfect one. She helps me remember my true nature, the one that is simply love and joy. As such, my goddess side is dealing with the choice to incarnate and learning to live in this sometimes perfect, sometimes imperfect world where there are all these constructs. One of the most powerful ones is gender.

What does it mean to be a woman, especially a woman on your own terms?

And when you remember you're really a goddess in a body, what does it mean to be a woman *then*?

I like to use the term goddess woman here. My experience is that once you realize you are a goddess woman, *everything* changes. You relate differently to yourself, your relationships, and the world around you.

Why? Because when you open yourself to experiencing divine love and joy in a body, it invariably translates into being a new woman somehow.

A goddess woman.

And you aren't the only one who will experience a changed perspective. Those who know and love you and those you encounter will relate to you differently too.

These guides are meant to share what my goddess nature has taught me and is still teaching me about being a woman. I've had many spiritual awakenings, but seeing myself as a goddess woman was one of the most powerful shifts I've ever experienced.

It happened when I was meditating on a full moon—no joke—and suddenly I saw myself lying naked on a lily pad on the water. That woman was beautiful, and I realized for the first time in my life that *I* was beautiful. Me! The girl who had always thought she was just okay looking but made up for it by being super smart and hard-working. I finally saw the woman some people had called "pretty."

She wasn't just pretty, though. She was beautiful and wise, sexy and confident, lying there naked.

Before that day, I had a lot of shame around my body, about not being skinny enough, not looking like whoever the most popular model or actress was at the time.

I also didn't have confidence in myself as a woman, one who knew she was perfect and loveable—just as she was.

From then on, whenever I looked in the mirror, I looked for *her*. Me, the Goddess Woman. I didn't find her everyday. Sometimes I was too distracted by a bad hair day or extra weight after the holidays. Sometimes I got caught up in doubts about myself or my decisions. But I never stopped looking for her. And you know what? The more I looked, the more I saw her.

Seeing her—that gorgeous goddess woman—gave me the courage to do things I never would have done. Including quitting a very successful career rebuilding warzones to launch myself as a published author. Including writing these guides, the topics of which rather astounded my woman-self. But my goddess nature knew what was best for me.

So does yours.

There is no order to reading the series of books that make up *The Goddess Guides to Being a Woman*. You will read them in the order your soul intends. Some guides may resonate more than others.

Each guide highlights a different divine formula. These formulas are recipes for love, happiness, and wholeness from our goddess woman selves that have gotten buried under a slew of personal experience, confusion about our true nature, and the insidious specter shame wreaks on our lives, on our very selves. Together, they form a path that will lead us to the fullest expression of our goddess woman selves.

We're also going to hear stories about goddess women and their journeys. We've been learning how to be goddess women for centuries through storytelling, much of it oral until recent times. The modern myths contained in these guides are composites of women everywhere, some of whom I've met, some of whom I've heard about. These stories are intended to demonstrate core lessons and elucidate wisdom to help all of us goddess women navigate our way through life.

But there is a flip side to stories—while they can provide guidance and share wisdom, so too can they keep us locked in unloving and unhappy patterns. The stories we tell ourselves again and again (even if they're not true), and the stories we take on from others, making them our own, can lead to a life and self very disconnected from our goddess nature. So we're going to spend some intentional time examining the stories we each carry (and the beliefs embedded in them) and identify the ones that are keeping us from feeling like we're goddesses in a body. Then we're going to delete them through what I call "Reclaiming Practices." As a goddess woman with spiritual healing gifts, I've learned this is one of the fastest and most effective ways to reconnect with and embody our goddess woman selves. By setting this unwanted baggage down, we can begin to experience love and joy as our normal course of being and live the highest version of our lives. We're also going to talk about a variety of goddess woman tools proven to support our goddess woman nature and journey.

Ultimately, your soul knows what you need if you're not certain. All you have to do is be willing to engage in this journey honestly and with as much love for yourself as you can muster. That's where the magic and miracles are, and they're waiting for you if you want them.

You need only ask.

No spiritual teacher worth his or her salt should ever profess to have all the truths of the Universe. I certainly don't. But I was called to write these guides, and I had help from above. One thing I've known since I started writing my first book many books ago is that I wasn't writing alone. When I surrendered to that truth, miraculous things happened. I changed. More readers found me. I hit the bestseller charts time and time again.

When you're a goddess woman living in alignment with her soul purpose, the whole Universe rises to support you, like you've heard before. The right people find you. You found me, and on a soul-level, I found you.

Listen to your intuition. It can never lead you wrong.

Since I'm a goddess learning how to be a woman—a goddess woman—the highest version of being a woman, not the crap I was taught or forced to believe—these guides are geared toward that experience. And for all the lesbians reading this, I encourage you to substitute female pronouns and the like wherever it's appropriate. My wording isn't meant to be exclusive. I'm only speaking from my experience as a heterosexual goddess woman.

Some of these truths will also resonate for men. We're all humans, after all. Again, while these guides are not meant to be exclusive, I'm going to confine myself to talking about goddesses and women, not gods and men. Those guides are meant to be written by a man who is called to share his truth. I wish him and the men in the world well. They need to remember who they are too.

In the meantime, though, it's going to be just us goddess women.

Happy reading and great spiritual shifting.

Much love and light,

Ava

Chapter 1

Reclaiming Our Divine Formula: Goddess+Swagger=Sexy

Sexy.

Pretty.

Beautiful.

Gorgeous.

Hot.

We throw these words around a lot. We've all heard them tagged to various women, the majority of them supermodels, singers, and actresses. Major magazines keep us apprised of the gold standard for beauty by issuing yearly lists of the sexiest and most beautiful women alive.

But how many of us would use all of those adjectives—heck, even one of them—to describe *ourselves*? This standard can feel impossible to live up to, but here's the thing—we don't need to. We are doing ourselves a disservice by trying.

Goddess women everywhere...Listen up.

Here's a divine truth for you to internalize: **You are PERFECT the way you were formed.**

You have the right eye color, the right hair color and texture, the right body type, the right legs, the right cheekbones, and the right skin color. The way you walk is perfect, and so is your voice. You get the drift. It's all perfect—for you.

You are unique and have gifts tailor-made for your goddess woman journey. No one can do what you can, be who you are. And that's your gift to the rest of us gods and goddesses in a body.

We are here to celebrate each other in this physical form, after all, and everything from the way you love, the way you think, the way you move, the way you dress, and the way you talk makes you a divine rockstar. And that includes women whose goddess bodies others might perceive as different—those who were born with disabilities, as well as those whose physical forms have been altered by either an accident or illness.

You are *all* love and joy and beauty and sexiness in a body. You were put here on this earth to rock it your way, with your own confidence. Your own swagger.

Why bring sexy back? When you choose to reclaim being a goddess woman, you're choosing to be the real you in physical form. No masks, no pretentions. No attempt to become a carbon copy of someone else. You know who you are. You trust yourself and your decisions, and that makes you confident. You came here with *everything* you need to live a divine rockstar life because you are a divine rockstar at the core.

Are you having trouble believing this is true? Having trouble wrapping your mind around it all? Thinking, but Ava, that's plumb crazy?

Most of us can't imagine this being true about ourselves. *We're* perfectly made? *We're* divine rockstars? With swagger? No f-ing way...

And the beautiful and sexy part? Seriously?

Okay, I hear you. It took me *years* to see and believe I was beautiful. Until recent months, I couldn't call myself "sexy" without blushing, laughing, and having my voice break. Right now, that only happens every once in a while when I focus on this reclamation.

And in case you're wondering, I'm still working on calling myself "hot" and "gorgeous" too, but I'm getting there. I'm clearing the stories that stand between me and reclaiming my sexy all the way.

Are you ready to reclaim yours? You're reading this, so some part of you wants it. Bad.

Some of you might be wondering, why are these words important at all in our journey as goddess women? Why do we *need* to feel sexy and beautiful and hot and gorgeous? To know we're divine rockstars?

Because we are goddesses in bodies. That means that in order to love ourselves fully, completely, we also need to love our bodies. And that translates to enjoying a loving self-image. Otherwise we're saying no to a full connection with our goddess woman selves.

If we don't believe we're beautiful or sexy, it affects every aspect of our lives. We might believe we're not good enough for this or that guy; that we're not going to get the job we want; that we're not desirable in bed with the lights on; that we'll be ridiculed or stared at in the community swimming pool by skinnier, more attractive women; or that we're not up to snuff when we look at our own visages in the mirror.

This type of thinking sends us down a rabbit hole of shame. We shrink. We withdraw. We disappear. We hide. We strike back. We lash out.

We become women we don't like, ones we wouldn't want to be.

To embrace ourselves as goddess women, we must also embrace our physicality.

Repeat after me: *Goddesses are sexy. All goddesses!*

Now, when I say "sexy," I'm not saying we're the kind of sex kittens or raunchy girls that we see permeating Western culture. Or the media's campaign to convince girls at younger and younger ages that they need to be sexy.

No, we're lush and hot and beautiful *as we are*. Everyone knows that no two people look entirely alike, and that's what makes us special.

Isn't it time we reclaimed that truth? Isn't it time we embraced ourselves as the divine rockstars we are?

How'd we get here?

Mainstream media and advertising and Photoshop are our jailers. And we've given them that power! We've been bamboozled by the notion that there are certain characteristics that make a woman sexy and beautiful. You've all seen and heard the same things I have. Images and articles telling us what we need to do, to *be*, to achieve perfection.

Some people even think women from certain countries are more beautiful than others. Can we say, Brazil, for example? And to achieve true sexiness, we're told we should be this weight, this height, this skin color, this type of breasts, these cheekbones, these eyes, this size of feet, and so on and so forth. Sometimes we're even told we're not physically healthy if we don't look like *their* images.

We start to buy into the story that we aren't sexy because we don't fit the bill. This way leads to madness. It's easy to start obsessing about the things we need to "fix" about our bodies, to buy into the notion that sexiness can only be achieved by looking outside ourselves, and to wait for someone else to affirm that we are beautiful.

It doesn't matter what culture you're in. Every culture has its own ideal, and it bears mentioning that sexiness—beauty, even—is culturally relative. As someone who has traveled the globe, I am incredibly attuned to this issue. And women in each country have key go-tos (exercise, surgery, body transformation, etc.) designed to make them beautiful and sexy according to this cultural ideal.

I have to admit that the following examples make me uncomfortable because these practices are about changing our bodies to fit outside standards about what's beautiful and sexy. Sure, we might be choosing it, but we're altering the inherent perfection of our goddess woman bodies. And we're giving away our power.

In Kenya, women scar their bodies in elaborate patterns; in Burma, they stretch their necks with gold rings; in Lebanon and Colombia, epic numbers have plastic surgery to change a nose, a brow line, cheekbones; in many Asian countries, women use creams or have surgeries like blepharoplasty to make their skin lighter and their eyelids flatter, something some analysts are starting to call a process of racial transformation. And if you think I'm leaving out my home country of the United States, wait for it. I live in a country obsessed by being thin and young. There are plenty of ways people alter their physical bodies to fit that standard through nip-and-tuck jobs, and that's only the tip of the iceberg.

Do all women buy into these cultural constructs about sexiness and beauty? No, but vast portions of us do, even though one essential truth about goddess women is that we aren't victims.

Even after all the reclaiming work I've done, I still go around with myself now and again, feeling the tug of the story that I'm not as sexy as so-and-so model or actress because I'm not thin enough or toned enough or classic enough. But I also immediately know it's a story, and I use my goddess power to stop it in its tracks.

Whether we're altering ourselves or critiquing ourselves in the mirror, that's shame snapping us up in its soul-crushing grip. It'll eviscerate our goddess woman nature in a heartbeat if we allow it.

Beyond the shame, which none of us want to invite into our lives, think of all the energy it saps from us to strive for these ideal types of sexiness and beauty. We make ourselves work out at the gym for reasons other than physical health; we pop diet pills; we starve ourselves; we spend a fortune on makeup and hair products and procedures; we obsess about our appearance. To what end? Wouldn't you rather pour this energy into being happy and playing with others you love?

And then there are the massive groups of women out there who have already admitted defeat in the pursuit of these ideals of beauty and sexiness. They cloak their bodies under baggy clothes, mired in shameful perceptions about their ugliness or their obesity.

This push-pull struggle is filling us with doubt, eroding our sense of self worth. We have forsaken personal acceptance, the soul-abiding knowledge of our perfection, burying it in the back of our consciousness like those "skinnier days" clothes in the back of the closet.

Why are we letting other people tell us who we are? Goddess women don't do that.

Your inner goddess is gently asking if you want to love yourself and this beautiful body you were given. She's asking if you want a fresh start. And it begins with remembering the divine formula you came wired with:

Goddess+Swagger=Sexy

Some of you are probably wondering what I mean by swagger. Prepare to let go of any negative stories you have about this term. This is *goddess* swagger.

The definition is simple: it's the fullest expression of you in your body, everything from the way you move, speak, dress, walk, and engage with others. It's the confidence you have in being a goddess in a body, one who can handle yourself in any situation you find yourself in because you embrace your uniqueness, a uniqueness that dances with the physical. It's the dignity you have from knowing you are worthy of both honor and respect as a woman.

And here's the key ingredient to goddess swagger... You have to believe it, so much so that you aren't just confident you're doing it, living it. You are it.

A woman with swagger knows she's beautiful with or without makeup; she feels as comfortable in bare feet as in heels; she wears what she wants to wear; she feels as confident in the bedroom as she does in the office; she relishes in her lush, pregnant body and the new life she's growing; she sings loudly because she loves to, not just when she's in the car or shower; she dances on the street if a band is playing and the mood strikes.

If you're still not sure how all of this could possibly apply to you, don't worry—we're going to talk a lot more about swagger. The sad truth is that I had trouble coming up with a known example of a woman with swagger, and I realized that's probably the point. But Denzel Washington easily came to mind for me. Why? We all know how he carries himself in his movies, whether he's playing the part of a former slave in *Glory* or a tough guy in *The Equalizer* or a football coach during the Civil Rights Movement in *Remember the Titans.* I'd bet he has swagger apart from acting, and it doesn't have anything to do with his looks. In the interviews I've seen, he talks about having a relationship to the Divine, and I used him as an example here because he's tapped into his god self. That's what we want to do. That's what we're doing here.

And it's going to look different for us as

women because we're different from men. Duality is a fact we live with every day. Our bodies are different. The nature of our roles is a little different, something that is deeply engrained in most of our stories. We have different "rules" about what it means to be a woman (something we're all being guided to revise for ourselves).

The bottom line is that while we were all born with swagger, most women just aren't taught that or even encouraged to embrace it. But that current reality doesn't make it any less true: goddesses have swagger. And it certainly doesn't mean that you can't reclaim it. You've already begun. Are you ready to go a little further?

Our divine formula is going to help us embrace how incredibly sexy and beautiful we are as goddess women. *Naturally.* Without all the fuss. Without all the enhancements. Does that mean I've started eschewing makeup or shaving my legs or dressing a certain way? Nope. I personally still like to do those things. Me, myself, and I.

And that's the point...

You're going to redefine beautiful and sexy for *you*. Not anyone else. That's your goddess transformation process, one we're all called to go through as goddess women.

And that can only come from a place of truly looking at how you are made and celebrating it—throwing off the shame-coated spectacles you've been wearing and seeing yourself with your new goddess woman eyes. Not criticizing and degrading yourself every time you look in the mirror. That's self-loathing behavior, not goddess woman behavior.

We also need to stop comparing ourselves to other goddess women. No more falling into the trap of believing someone is prettier, sexier, better looking than we are and trying to look or be like they are. They're just made differently, maybe celebrated differently in the world. Don't you remember the old adage, "Beauty is in the eye of the beholder?"

Am I talking crazy? No. It's possible. If I can do it, anyone can.

You simply have to choose to take it back.

Are you going to have moments when you look at your belly and cringe a little, wishing it were flatter (or whatever makes you cringe)? Sure. I do. But we'll know what to do in those moments: clear the shame and reaffirm our self-acceptance.

I love and accept myself. I am perfect as I am.

But do you know what else we need to do? We need to throw off all the stories holding us back from claiming our swagger: ones like you can't be sexy and spiritual, smart and sexy, successful and sexy in business. Those stories are eroding our goddess nature too.

Our bodies are the vehicles of our divine selves. They are the embodiment of the light and miracle we are in the Universe. It's no accident that scientists say we are made from star dust. When was the last time you called a star in the midnight sky "ugly?" Said it wasn't blinking bright enough? Probably never.

Stars are radiant. Brilliant. Beautiful. They captivate us. They awe us. They open us up to the magnificence of the Universe.

Why would you as a goddess woman be any different?

Are you ready to get your swagger back? See that everything that makes you up is beautiful, sexy, gorgeous, hot, and pretty? Maybe for the first time in your whole life?

Heck yeah, you are.

CHAPTER 2

THE BIG SHUT DOWNS TO SEXY AND SWAGGER

Someone shut down your goddess swagger early on, made you believe you either weren't beautiful and sexy or that you were nothing more than that. You stopped expressing yourself *your way* in *your* body.

Basically, someone convinced you that you weren't a divine rockstar.

And, for whatever reason, you let them. Maybe you trusted their opinion. Maybe other people started using the same spirit-crushing epithets about you because "birds of a feather flock together." Suddenly, your personal experience began to overtake your divine knowledge.

You developed stories around what it meant

to be a woman, how you needed to look and act and dress and be. Maybe something happened that made you feel unsafe about being sexy. You might have been punished for it. You might have been shamed. Or you might have been subjected to one of the most egregious offenses that can be done to any goddess woman: rape or sexual abuse.

No matter how you got here, trust me when I say you are going to get your goddess swagger back if you want it. Like we discuss in detail in *Goddesses Decide*, choice is the key to your goddess power.

All over the world, goddess women have been shut down and are still being shut down when it comes to letting their sexy out. We're going to tackle some of the most common shut downs and say goodbye to them.

SHUT DOWN #1:

Feeling Judged

Do you remember the first time you felt judged? Told you weren't pretty or special?

This starts when we're young usually. Perhaps one of your parents insisted you wear a stocking hat before going out because your ears were too big. Perhaps an older sibling said she was prettier because you were chubby. Perhaps, like me, you wore hand-me-down or homemade clothing and were ridiculed by the other kids at school and called ugly. Perhaps a teacher said you were a hot mess after you came in from playing at recess and told you not to swing anymore because your skirt came up and your hair got all wild—not lady-like.

If you believed them, the judgments that were leveled at you became part of your story. The inherent shame in the barbs and criticisms penetrated your goddess woman spirit and made you feel less, feel small. Maybe the judgments even made you alter your behavior. Perhaps you didn't dress the same way anymore after your grandfather told you he could see through your blouse. Maybe you stopped wearing the red Chanel lipstick you loved so much, had saved up to buy in high school, after one of your classmates said you looked like a slut.

I have yet to meet a woman who doesn't

have a story about something someone said about her looks, the way she dressed, or the way she talked or acted. I find it very interesting that even some of the so-called most beautiful women in the world share stories like these in interviews.

Like we discussed in *Goddesses Don't Do Drama*, it's impossible to live in a bubble (and who would want to?). We're going to come into contact with other people, and people who are not living their god or goddess nature might say mean things about us for whatever reason. The point is that there *is* judgment. And some women are downright judgmental of other women. How many times have you heard a man say, "You women are vicious to each other?"

The judgment comes not from fellow goddess women, but from women who are still locked in their own stories and perhaps hate themselves, their bodies, their choices, and their lives on some level. That being said, knowing this doesn't always soften the barb or the dagger they throw your way. Words can hurt.

We as goddess women need to face the fact

that judgment exists so we can stand in our goddess woman shoes when it happens to us. When someone looks at us with judgment when we walk into a restaurant and whispers about our love handles showing or our blouse revealing too much cleavage, we don't let it penetrate our goddess robes. We know who we are. We *love* who we are.

We own it.

But it's not just the judgment of other people that keeps us from being comfortable in our own skin.

For me, religious stories about the so-called evils of being sexy and the inherent shame of *wanting* to feel this way corrupted my own self-image. Crappy stories were told to me by religious figures and people I trusted (parents, grandparents, teachers, etc.) about sexy girls being promiscuous, getting into trouble, blah, blah, blah.

These so-called sexy women were reviled for being "evil" in some cases, for leading men to their doom. Think of all the literature and paintings that depict women as sirens, seductresses: Homer's *Odyssey*,

Gone With The Wind by Margaret Mitchell, Vladimir Nabokov's *Lolita*, *The Fall of Man and the Expulsion from Paradise* by Michelangelo, *Venus of Urbino* by Titian, and Klimt's *Salome*. And we're just getting started. How about some historical femme fatales? We're talking Lilith, Mata Hari, and Cleopatra.

This is a full-on archetype, goddess women, and it doesn't serve any of us. But let's bring it back to the present, shall we?

I don't know about your world, but in mine girls who went to church weren't supposed to be sexy. Neither were girls who went to Catholic schools like I did. Perhaps that's why the nuns mandated we all wear the same plain uniform. People were punished for showing their bodies, even a little leg—girls whose skirts didn't pass the ruler tests (a.k.a. anything that skimmed above the knee) were given detention. The girls who were sexy in Catholic school were "bad" and "loose"—a reputation that led kids in public school to half-jokingly refer to my high school as Mount St. Mattress. Nice, right? It was mortifying to meet public school boys and have them give me a leer when they heard where I went to school.

My family moved to the South after my formative years, and I found myself staring a new and unfamiliar feminine ideal in the face: the Southern beauty queen. Women put on makeup to go to a gym class composed of other women, came home and showered, and put it on all over again—something I didn't understand or feel was practical for me. I can't tell you how many times I'd go for a run and encounter a woman who'd say, "Oh, you have the loveliest skin." Since I was an outsider, I thought they were complimenting me until a home-grown friend laughed and told me they were shaming me for not wearing makeup when I was in public. Hmm... Come to think of it, those comments usually started with "Bless your heart."

As I grew older, I felt more and more tangled up in a mishmash of stories about what it meant to be pretty and sexy and beautiful. I was flat-out confused about what this looked like for me and when (if ever) I could achieve it.

And I'm not the only one. Friends who didn't go to church or consider themselves spiritual or Southern still wrestled with these issues, these stories, even these archetypes. They are pervasive and destructive and are still controlling how we as goddess women feel about our bodies and express ourselves through our bodies.

Let's get rid of this shit...

Reclaiming Practice Intro

If you've read any of the other *Goddess Guides to Being a Woman*, you know this is the time when we pull out what I like to call the Goddess Blaster. It's a tool we use to pretty much blast out the stories we're believing so we can reconnect with our goddess woman truth. If you're a pro, move on ahead. If you're doing this for the first time, here's a little more about how transformative these practices can be.

Think of your mind as a computer. The stories you believe are the software you've added to your personal computer. Maybe you've even thrown in an app or two. The stories that keep you locked in patterns or judgments can be cleared by simply calling them out there with intention, repetition, and commitment. It's like you're deleting the code that isn't making you feel happy or giving you the kind of goddess self and life you want. You can utilize this tool anytime your goddess self makes you aware of a story you're buying into.

How about we dive right into the first one so you can see what I mean?

RECLAIMING PRACTICE #1:

Erasing Judgments

I want you to take a moment. Think about the kinds of things people have said about you that have hurt your feelings. Did someone say you were fat? Has everyone always said it? Did someone say you'd be lucky to ever get married because you were ugly? Did someone say your style was way too sexy for your neighborhood, and you needed to tone it down?

There are truckloads of judgments you've probably heard about your body and about you as a woman. Let your goddess self help you hear them. It's okay to feel the hurt. It did hurt. It does hurt.

And if you're pissed off? Yeah. How could they say that to you? How could they be so cruel?

Let a few faces rise in your consciousness. Who said the hurtful remarks? How did you feel? What happened after they said it?

Your goddess nature is going to show you the big judgments and events that need to be cleared.

Repeat after me:

All of the horrible things people said about me and my body, I transmute and clear them.

All the ways they made me feel like shit, like I was nothing, like I wasn't pretty or strong or sexy or beautiful, I transmute and clear them.

All the ways I don't believe I'm pretty, beautiful, sexy, or have swagger, I transmute and clear them.

All of the junk I believe about what it means to be sexy or to be pretty, I transmute and clear it.

All of the junk I believe about what a woman should be like, I transmute and clear it.

My belief that there is only one way to be beautiful, I transmute and clear it.

All of the ways I changed how I acted or looked at myself, I transmute and clear them.

They have no power over me anymore.

I say no to their opinions. I will not believe them anymore. I will not take them into me.

I want you to take one of the people who came up for you, who you might put on a Most Wanted list. If you're ready to forgive them, let's do it. If you're not there yet, you can just bless them. Or you can skip ahead. The choice is always yours.

To the person who hurt or angered you the most, please say:

X (Name), all of the stories we have together, I transmute and clear them.

You hurt me. But I forgive you in this moment. I don't want to carry this anymore.

I am a goddess woman, and I choose to be free.

We need never cross paths again.

But if we do, we're not going to create any more stories like this.

I release my part in this, and I bless you and wish you well.

If you have other people on your Most Wanted list, you can go through this practice again. Or if another memory or story to clear comes up later, simply circle back to it and delete it.

How about we put on our Big Brave and look at the ways we criticize *ourselves*? We're going to spend a little more time on this later, but there's a lot to clear here. The sooner we start, the better. Let's clear some of it now.

All my tendencies to be my own cruelest judge, I transmute and clear them.

All the ways I won't give myself a break or love myself and my body, I transmute and clear them.

Take a breath. That was huge. I know it raised up a lot of emotion; it did for me too. But you're freeing yourself up, one affirmation at a time.

We're going to move along to the next shut down.

Shut Down #2:

Being Punished

Make no mistake, punishment is meant to be a corrective tool, and it's pretty effective. When we experience punishment, it wounds us deeply and can leave a lasting impression. And the punishment can run the gamut from shaming, shunning, hazing, "hating," and denying. In *Goddesses Cry and Say Motherfucker*, we discussed the harm punishment can do to our ability to freely express ourselves; goddess women are also punished for being beautiful, sexy, and having swagger.

A girl gets sent to her room by her mom for wearing a mini-skirt after she was told to change; a middle-school girl is bullied by classmates because she doesn't wear a bra yet; a teenager doesn't get into the college of her choice because the admissions staff found an unauthorized naked picture of her online; a college student refuses to sleep with her professor to improve her grade and gets an F in the class; a wife gets the cold shoulder from her husband after a party because other men were ogling her cleavage in the dress her husband had told her was too revealing; a working woman gets called out by her boss for "showing too much skin at work"; a middle-aged woman's daughter shames her for dressing and acting like a cougar after her husband left her.

Being punished for being a woman, for being pretty or sexy or beautiful, can make a goddess woman not want to be in her body. And no body, no swagger. The flip side is true as well. Maybe she's punished because she isn't perceived as being pretty or sexy or beautiful enough.

A mother sends her tomboy-daughter girl to her room because she won't wear the dress she bought her; a teacher takes away a snack from a student because she's "had enough"; a husband tells his wife she can't spend any more money on clothes until she loses weight; a dancer doesn't get the lead role because her jaw is too "masculine."

Many of us have been punished, at different times in our lives, for *both* of these things (for being perceived as sexy *and* for not being pretty enough). How's that for mixed messages?

What do we do when this happens to us? We might try to correct the reason for the punishment. Or perhaps we decide to rebel. Regardless, if we believe on some level we either deserved to be punished for the action or will be punished again, we will likely do everything we can to prevent it. When we fall into this trap, we stop expressing our natural goddess woman selves. We're letting other people steal our swagger.

Let's get it back...

RECLAIMING PRACTICE #2:

Throwing Off the
Chains of Punishment

What is your story here? What is the one punishment for being perceived as too sexy or not sexy enough that has really stuck with you all these years? Maybe it's one you still dream about. Maybe it's one you fear will happen again. Or maybe it's your ongoing hell, something that repeats over and over again.

Let's throw off the chains of the stories that have held us back from our divine formula.

All the ways I was punished for being pretty or sexy or beautiful, I transmute and clear them.

All of the ways I was punished for being fat or ugly or disgusting, I transmute and clear them.

Everything they said to me, I transmute and clear it.

Everything they did to me, I transmute and clear it.

All the ways it hurt, I transmute and clear them.

All the ways it shut me down, I transmute and clear them.

All the times I couldn't stop it from happening, I transmute and clear them.

All the times they wouldn't listen to me or see my

side of things, I transmute and clear them.

I refuse to believe what you said to me. I love myself. I believe in myself. I won't let you do it anymore. It ends now. I am a goddess woman. I am love and joy. If you can't see that, it's not my fault. I won't be bound or punished by your limited or twisted opinion of me.

Again, take one of the main characters in your story. Maybe it's the one you fear the most. If you want to forgive and let them go, how about we do so right now?

X (Name), I forgive you for what you said to me, for hurting me, for punishing me, for making me cry, for doubting myself, for making me rage. I release you to live your life, and I bless you. I plan to live mine. We don't need to do this again. It is done.

Again, punishment doesn't always come from the outside. Some of the harshest criticism can come from our own egos. How have you punished yourself for not being pretty or sexy or beautiful? Or for thinking you're ugly or fat or undesirable?

All the reasons I punish myself, I transmute and

clear them.

All the reasons I push myself to be skinnier or prettier or sexier or younger, I transmute and clear them.

We're going to talk about how you feel about your body in more detail, so don't worry if you feel you still have a ways to go. Loving yourself in your body is a process, but you've already started the hard work. Take a breath. Even if it doesn't feel that way right now, you're changing your life. We're just wading through all the shit in your shit bucket, as I like to say. Every unloving thought you believe—whether it's from you or someone else—is a piece of shit. No one wants a huge bucket full of—well, shit—but it builds up when you carry it around and don't let it go. But you *are* letting it go, and your goddess self is cheering you on big time.

Ready for the next shut down? We're getting into disturbing, epic territory here, and it seems like the insults to our very goddess woman selves are only escalating. Thanks for taking the next step.

Shut Down #3:

Feeling Unsafe

What was the first time you felt unsafe being a girl, a woman?

Did a boy grab a part of your body when you were starting to develop? Did a teacher look at you strangely after class and brush up against your body, his breath hot in your ear? Did a man follow you out of the gym to your car after telling you he thought you were hot?

Maybe it wasn't one moment for you, but a persistent sensation. You live(d) in an unsafe situation, perhaps with an abusive parent or in a dangerous neighborhood.

If you have never felt unsafe as a woman, congratulations, you've been starring in a pretty great goddess woman script. I personally only know one woman who hasn't felt this way—my BFF—but judging from all the stories other goddess women have shared with me during my life, she is a rare example.

I'd like to say that most of the moments

when I felt unsafe were when I was traveling to dangerous countries for my old career (rebuilding warzones), but the fact is I've had plenty of moments like this here at home, in a supposedly developed country. My old stories were riddled with experiences of feeling unsafe in my goddess body. The result? I did whatever I could to dim down any interest prurient boys or men might have in me as a woman.

My first shut down came when the boys started grabbing my newly developing breasts in middle school. Those moments in class or on the playground terrified me on a primal level my female nature hadn't connected to before. There was shock they would touch me, my body, a private part of me like my breasts. I was still getting used to them, and all the attention made me even more ashamed of them.

Later on, I would feel unsafe when I walked by a construction site and all the men would pause and catcall and whistle at me. Hearing them say they wanted to "fuck me" always had me hurrying across the street and sagging with relief when I was out of their line of vision.

I didn't believe this kind of male behavior would change or that I could do anything to change it, mostly because of how often it was (and is) accepted with impunity. You know, that whole "boys will be boys" crap. And the prevalence of the backward notion that women are at fault for getting this kind of attention/abuse because they're sexy isn't helping anyone. It's keeping many of us from facing this behavior straight on and saying it's wrong, that it needs to stop.

Are any memories floating up for you? Maybe you buried them, or maybe you haven't thought about them in a while; maybe this just happened to you yesterday.

It's the way a teenage bully leers at you when you're wearing a mini-skirt at school; when you're in a parking lot at night going to your car and a group of boys calls out about "showing you a good time"; when you're running or walking on a nature path and you cross paths with a man, only to realize moments later that he's changed directions and is behind you; when your boss says you have beautiful hair and touches it.

That feeling of being unsafe makes most of us want to hide—hide our bodies or our hair, hide our beauty, hide what makes us sexy and unique, what gives us swagger. Pretty much hide everything about us.

It completely sucks. It creates fear. If it's traumatic, it's something you're on guard against. You might not wear a certain outfit anymore or make your eyes dark and smoky for a night out. You might start to wear baggier or more androgynous clothes. You might even cut your hair to be less long and lustrous. I danced with these strategies for well over a decade until I decided I didn't want to be afraid of being a woman anymore, of being scared that being a woman was going to attract attention I didn't want.

If you've ever felt like this, come with me. We're going to clear it so you don't have to be afraid anymore.

RECLAIMING PRACTICE #3:

Upending the Fear

There's a lot of emotion building here. I can

feel it. This one is going to release a lot, so take some deep breaths and put your hand over your heart.

Repeat after me:

All the ways I feel unsafe or felt unsafe being a woman, being sexy, being pretty, being me, I transmute and clear them.

All the fear I had in that moment and still carry, I transmute and clear it.

All the ways I'm on guard, I transmute and clear them.

All the reasons it happened, I transmute and clear them.

All the ways I blame myself, or wonder if I did something to cause it or why I wasn't smart enough to see it coming, I transmute and clear them.

All the blame I level at myself for not stopping it from happening, I transmute and clear it.

All the anger I feel that I was just going along and living my life and this jerk frightened me, I transmute and clear it.

All the ways it's made me change where I go or how I act or dress, I transmute and clear them.

I forgive myself for believing being sexy, being a woman makes me unsafe.

I allow myself to feel free again to be a woman in the world.

Think about the person or persons involved. Did you know them? Did you simply come across them? Let's send them on their way too.

The person or people who made me feel unsafe, I transmute and clear them.

The person or people who made me doubt I was safe in my body, in my community, at my job, at the gym—in the world—I transmute and clear them.

Whatever your reasons or intentions, you made me feel unsafe as a woman. But I'm not going to let you win. I'm not going to let fear change me or rule my life. I am going to be free. I am going to be my goddess woman self. I am going to dress like I want, act like I want, walk like I want. I will go anywhere I feel called to go, because I listen to my goddess nature, and she would never put me in an unsafe situation. We are so in tune with each other, I will hear everything she needs to tell me. I can trust I am safe. But I don't need to repeat this situation or these events. I release myself from them for all time.

Whew! I'll bet there's a buildup of emotion in your gut or your chest, maybe even your throat. Let's take some deep breaths—as big as you can breathe—and let all of this go. Keep breathing until you feel ready to move on.

I also feel like we should spend a little time clearing any worries you may carry for the other women you love. I feel like some of you worry for your friends, sisters, mothers, daughters, grandbabies. We don't want to put our stories or any fear from our experiences on them.

All my worries about X (Name) being safe when she goes out, I transmute and clear them.

All the reasons I'm afraid about X happening, I transmute and clear them.

How are we feeling? Goodness, this is big stuff, goddess women. Breathe. Feeling unsafe is a huge shut down for goddess women. But we have one more to face, and you'll know if you need to read the next section or can skip ahead.

SHUT DOWN #4:

Violence

If you've had violence done toward your body in the form of rape, date rape, assault, sexual harassment, stalking, domestic violence, or sexual abuse (intended or attempted violence), there's been some serious trauma dealt to your goddess woman nature. To simply refer to it as another shut down seems unfair and shortsighted. It's a hell of a lot more than that, isn't it?

I could go into some of the statistics I've heard—one in three women in the United States have been raped or date raped; one in ten women in the United States have experienced sexual abuse; immigrant women in the United States have higher incidents of rape than non-immigrants; in Africa, women experience rape at least three times in their lifetime; and countries with some of the highest reported rapes include South Africa, Botswana, Sweden, Nicaragua, Pakistan, and Panama.

Honestly, these are only known cases. I've had plenty of friends tell me they were raped or abused and never reported it. I don't think we know how many women in the world have experienced violence against their person. All we know is that it's a huge number and it's wrong. It's illegal. It's a crime.

Like I said in *Goddesses Love Cock*, crimes against our bodies, ones that seem to target us as women, cause emotional, psychological, physical, and mental anguish. If you have experienced this and are still dealing with the effects, I highly recommend working with a professional.

As someone who's experienced assault attempts, I can share that it's taken many years of intentional work to overcome their effects. Post-traumatic stress and I have been friends for a long, long time, and I'm happy to share I'm mostly over it. Sure, I still have some triggers, but I also have plenty of reclaiming tools.

I wish you healing in whatever shape it needs to take. I know the Universe and your goddess woman self is with you, helping you. But we're also going to invite in whatever healing and reclaiming can happen *now*. I believe every moment contains the miracle of healing if we want it, if we ask for it.

I'm also going to say that if you've ever been aggressively kissed or fondled by a man you didn't give permission to, for example, you've experienced violence to your goddess woman self too. I could give more examples, but you're going to know if you felt like you were in danger for being a woman. We don't need to get into degrees of violence.

Violence against our bodies is wrong and harmful and makes us doubt our goddess woman nature on a core level. Let's release some of this right now.

RECLAIMING PRACTICE #4:

Ultimate Freedom

I want you to think of a moment or an event

that is still haunting you, one that still has its hooks in you.

Your head might be hurting right now from all the trauma or your chest might be super tight. Take a deep breath with me. You can do this. We're in this together. I'm right here, and so is your goddess self. She's got you.

Repeat after me:

All the ways I still think about it—and can't stop—I transmute and clear them.

All the ways I wish it had never happened, I transmute and clear them.

All the ways I wish I could have stopped it, I transmute and clear them.

All the ways I don't understand why it had to happen to me, I transmute and clear them.

All the ways I don't understand what I did to deserve it, I transmute and clear them.

All the shame and fear it brings to mind, I transmute and clear it.

All my fears that I'll never get over it, feel safe again, feel like myself again, I transmute and clear them.

All my fear someone will find out, I transmute and clear it.

All my fear it will happen again, I transmute and clear it.

All my fear no one will understand, I transmute and clear it.

All the times my story has scared other people, I transmute and clear them.

All of the places I'm scared to go to now, I transmute and clear them.

All of the people I'm scared to be around, I transmute and clear them.

Everywhere I'm jumpy, can't sleep, afraid to date, afraid to have sex, afraid to see my family, I transmute and clear them.

Everything else that is ready to be released right now, I transmute and clear them.

I am whole. I am loved. I am safe. I am brave for

being here. I am brave for being me. I am brave for getting up and walking out of the house, walking into the world.

I don't know if you've been able to forgive the person or people involved yet. It's always your choice. I needed some time to get over how angry I was, but I ultimately decided I didn't want to carry any of that emotion anymore. If you want to go a little deeper with forgiveness today, repeat after me:

X (Name if you know it), I don't know why you hurt me. I didn't deserve it. Part of me wants to hate you, but I'm going to let that go. I forgive you. I'm not making excuses for what you did. It was wrong. I ask for justice, divine justice, and divine compensation for the pain and suffering I endured. I ask that x, y, and z (my innocence, a feeling of safety, my health—whatever you want) be restored to me. I release you for all time. We will never cross paths again.

If you feel like crying, that's okay. I feel a little like crying too. I'm remembering some of my own experiences.

Cry it out if you need to. Pace. Hug yourself.

Remembering all of this and releasing it is a brave act, a goddess act. Do something nice for yourself. You loved yourself big time today.

And you reclaimed more of your goddess woman self.

Bravo, brave heart!

CHAPTER 3

SOUL-LEECHING STEREOTYPES

Now that we've named and cleared some of our biggest shut downs to feeling sexy and beautiful in our goddess woman bodies, we're going to tackle what I call soul-leeching stereotypes.

There's no beating around the bush with these stories. When I started to compile a list of the ones I've come across in my life experience (and/or heard about from friends), I got a little overwhelmed, frankly. These were the kind of stories that invade a culture's psyche so deeply that they become stereotypes. Almost truth. The kind of thing that will make someone say, "I don't want to believe it's that way, but there is so much evidence to say that it is."

These are not stereotypes like "trophy wife" or "cat lady," but fuller "story" stereotypes that undermine our ability to embody and express our truest and fullest goddess woman selves. They are the kind of tropes that become the basis for popular TV shows, movies, and books. They are the kind of stereotypes that keep us in bondage.

Of course, stereotypes can become self-fulfilling prophesies. When we buy into them, we make them true, halting our embodiment of our goddess woman selves. I starkly remember one night at a professional women's group I was invited to in Washington, D.C. A lawyer told me I'd never get married unless I dumbed myself down and acted like a sexy little kitten; that's what had finally snagged her the successful husband, the house, and the kids she'd always wanted. Men were threatened by smart women, she said. I was also told, "Giggle more and don't share your opinions." Other women agreed with her, and I found myself being barraged by their advice.

What was the most shocking to me was the fact that most of the women were college-educated and were working in law, medicine, politics, business, etc., likely bringing in over six figures. But they didn't believe they could be loved for being smart. That they could be seen as sexy without pretending to be someone else.

I never went back to this group, but it showed me how insidious stories can take root and start to spread. These women were trying to help me because I was single (one of the few in that group at the time), but they were basically telling me I couldn't be loved by a man for being me. They couldn't, so why would I, right?

And I imagine they gave this same message to all the other single women they encountered. Maybe someone else listened to all of those successful, (supposedly) happily married women with the big houses and families. She might have believed they'd struck upon a magic formula. She might have stopped believing she was a goddess woman—beautiful and sexy without any need to change for anyone.

Goddess women need to be liberated from this bullshit, straight up.

Let's run through a few of these stereotypes and see what pings you. Maybe someone said something to you and you started to believe it. Maybe your goddess self has been waiting for the veil to be removed from your eyes. You might want to grab a pen and paper and write down some additional ones that come up for you.

Get ready to be uncomfortable. Here are some of the cruel things people say. I'm cringing as I write them.

Smart Girls Don't Bag Men

No man wants to be with a woman who's smarter than he is. You have to act stupid, like you don't have a care in the world. Throw your head back and giggle more. That's the kind of woman a man wants.

Sleeping-Your-Way-To-The-Top Phenomena

If she got somewhere, it's because she used sex or her sex appeal to get there. I'll bet she slept with her boss. Maybe more than one. She didn't get that job or that promotion on her own merit.

Sexy Women Aren't Respected

They only get by on their tits and ass. Everyone knows that. What could they possibly have to say that's interesting? No one takes them seriously.

Sexy Women Can't Be Successful Outside the Entertainment Industry

They're selling sex. That's their job. You can't be sexy in a serious profession.

Sexy Women Can't Be Trusted

They will steal your man. They will compete with you to get a man. They will cut you in a heartbeat over a man.

Sexy Women Are Asking for It

Otherwise, why would they dress like that? Look like that? Act like that?

Don't Hate Me Because I'm Beautiful

I'm better than you. I'm more beautiful, sexier, etc. I'm somehow more perfectly made than the rest of you people, and it's not my fault. I've just got better genes than you, more beautiful parents.

Fat Girls Are Lazy

They let themselves go. They don't apply themselves. I mean, look at them.

Fat Girls Are Unhealthy

There must be something physically wrong with you to be this fat. It's not normal. Especially if you're young.

You're Pretty for a Big Girl

You're obviously doing something different than the others. You're not so bad.

Hot Guys Don't Want Fat Girls

They're hot. Why would they want you?

Moms Aren't Hot

I can never be sexy again. I'm never going to look good again.

Good Moms Shouldn't Be Sexy

They're like, moms. They're supposed to be role models. Not look like a woman some guy wants to fuck. They should be beyond that.

Wives Can't Be Sexy

They're obviously looking to have an affair. Otherwise, why would they dress like that?

Spiritual People Aren't Sexy

You can't be. I mean, you're supposed to be above all that body stuff. It fades. It's not important. Holy people shouldn't want to look good.

Sexy People Aren't Spiritual

They're shallow. What do they know of real human suffering? They've had it easy. They only care about their looks. Nothing meaningful.

Ugly Girls Don't Have Friends

No one wants to be around them. They don't think enough of themselves to try to look better, more attractive.

Women Who Think Too Much of Themselves Are Arrogant

They're too big for their britches. Who told them they were so great? They are a disgrace to all women, suggesting they're better than everyone else.

Women Who Say What They Want and Go for It Are Bitches

They're loudmouthed. Aggressive. They don't care about anyone but themselves. They'll step on anyone to get to the top.

She's A Man-eater

She eats men for breakfast, lunch, and dinner. She fucks them and throws them out like garbage.

She's A Ball Buster

She gets off on taking men down and putting them in their place. She's got a pair. She really wishes she had a dick.

You're Ancient—Stop Trying to be Sexy, Grandma

Stop trying to wear that. Do your hair like that. You're not seventeen anymore. You're wrinkly and dry. Not sexy.

Are you feeling a little ill? Are you remembering a time when someone said something like this to you? Have you said something like this to someone else?

Were there any other stories that came up for you? My head is about ready to explode. Let's blast away these suckers.

RECLAIMING PRACTICE #5:

Stopping the Stereotypes Invasion

Let's start with a general clearing.

All the ways I'm shocked by these stereotypes, I transmute and delete them.

All the ways they feel cruel and hurtful, I transmute and delete them.

All the stories I've heard about being smart, sexy, ugly, or fat, I transmute and delete them.

All the stories about what it means to be successful, I transmute and delete them.

All the stories about being spiritual, I transmute and delete them.

All the ways women can't be smart, sexy, and confident, and are called names like bitch or slut, I transmute and delete them.

All of the shame I feel because of these stories, I transmute and delete it.

If there were certain stories that made you sick or uncomfortable, why don't you take one of them right now? We'll clear it specifically together.

All the stories about X, I transmute and delete them.

All the ways I believe(d) this, I transmute and delete them.

All the ways I lived this, I transmute and delete them.

All the ways I acted because of this, I transmute and delete them.

All the ways I've tried but failed to escape them, I transmute and delete them.

All the ways they make me want to run and hide, I transmute and delete them.

All the ways they make me want to hit back, strike back, I transmute and delete them.

Take a few of your more sickness-inducing stories and run through this exercise again. It's okay if you're feeling vulnerable. You were hurt. It's okay to feel the sadness come up. And if you're getting angry, remembering all the barbs and jabs you've endured, take a moment and breathe with me. You might also be getting upset because you're so tired of people throwing around stereotypes like this. You understand they cause harm, and you want it to stop.

Breathe. Repeat after me:

All of the emotion I'm feeling right now, I transmute and delete it.

I let it go. I don't need to carry it anymore.

These stories are done for me. For all time.

Whew! That was a lot of energy. Do you feel how tight your chest is? You might even be buzzing. I know I am. Take a breath. Let's dig a little deeper. Are there any particular faces coming to mind with these stories? Bullies? Loved ones? How about we let go of them too, at least insofar as they made us feel this way? Only if you're ready... Your choice.

X (Name), I forgive you for the role you played for me. Go in peace.

I thank you. I bless you. This is done. For all time.

And if you're upset with yourself because you believed those stories or stereotypes were true of *you*, and it made your life go a certain way, let's just be loving to ourselves.

All the decisions I made for me and my life because I believed this crap, I transmute and delete them.

I love myself. I accept myself.

I forgive myself for ever believing I was wrong

or bad or less because of these stories, these lies.

Maybe you remember saying things like this about other people or to other people, or thinking them. How about we clear that out too? Was there someone in your life you judged harshly because you believed these stereotypes? Perhaps your stories got tangled up somewhere along the way. Maybe your husband left you for a woman who seemed younger and sexier; maybe he even told you that was the reason.

All the times I criticized other women for being sexy or smart or fat or confident or old or spiritual, I transmute and delete them.

All the times I made fun of X (name) for being X, I transmute and delete them.

The people we criticize have been hurt like we have. These are cruel stories. It's hard to admit words hurt, especially for those of us who were brought up to believe another idiom/stereotype: "sticks and stones may break my bones, but words will never hurt me." But we're human too and having people treat us like this is sometimes shocking to our goddess nature.

Let's agree to set aside our knives and pledge to look for the good in other women moving forward. Maybe we might even feel called to say something kindly to stop other people from perpetuating these stories.

Goddess Woman Declaration

Celebrating All
Goddess Women

I, (Name,) hereby declare that I am willing to see the inner goddess in every woman I encounter. I am willing to let my goddess nature tap me on the shoulder when my ego invents judgments against another woman because of how she looks, dresses, acts, or simply walks in the world.

I agree to use kind and loving words to other goddess women, including myself. I agree to celebrate them and their path. I agree to encourage them to be sexy and confident and smart and wonderful—everything they decide makes them happy and loved.

I celebrate all goddess women and their swagger.

Great job! You just changed your world. And the other goddess women you come into contact with will never be the same.

Ready for the next step? Let's jump in.

CHAPTER 4

REBELLION OR ASSIMILATION

When we come into contact with events and/or stories that threaten to shut down our goddess nature, a particular brand of behavior often takes root. We might choose full-on rebellion against these events and/or stories, against society itself. But if we believe the cost is too great for us to live our goddess woman nature, we might choose assimilation instead. Either way, we get tugged out of our goddess woman selves, encouraged to become something else. Another woman.

For some of us it becomes a pattern that plays out in our lives.

Rebellion

Anger and opposition are the rebel's part-ners. It's their f-you to the people who judge them to be lesser, who make them feel wrong or powerless or bad. This is the girl or woman who smokes, even though she knows it's unhealthy, to flaunt her inde-pendence; the girl who stays out all night to party and drink even though she'd rather curl up with a book; who flirts with bad boys and situations she knows aren't good for her; or the one who consistently wears a mini-skirt just inches below her crotch to church service.

Rebels make it their mission to upset the apple cart at every turn. They're hurting deep on the inside, and that hurt expresses itself as anger. (Remember the formula mentioned in *Goddesses Cry and Say Mother-fucker*? Unexpressed Hurt=Anger) Call these girls or women onto the carpet? They'll say, "Fuck you." Set a stupid rule designed to control them? They won't just break it; they'll get in your face about it to make you as uncomfortable as you made them.

Maybe they're hoping to preserve a shred

of what they believe is their individualism until they can leave their small-minded communities. Maybe they're daring someone to love them, even with the chip on their shoulder, the purple hair, the tattoos, and the nose ring.

How about a story?

My BFF was part of a conservative Persian family who came to the United States when she was a baby. Girls were expected to be obedient and not talk back. You went to school, were an excellent student, got a good job, and then got married. That was the expected path. Boys did not exist until you met your husband, who your family likely chose for you.

Her dad was especially strict. From the time she was a toddler, she couldn't play with other children or go to their houses because they were "bad" influences. They would make her do bad things: smoking, drinking, drugs, sex. No one outside the family could be trusted. Needless to say, her parents were her main moral authority. Her dad taught her to think for herself when she was in the world, like observing her teachers and watching for "bad" influences.

The more time she spent in the outside world, the more the story her parents had told her about outside influences started to break down. Largely due to the fact that her dad had, ironically enough, taught her to think for herself.

She realized not every family was like hers. She saw that some of her parents' friends were the "bad" people her parents had told her to stay away from. The friends she met in school and in the neighborhood were nice, not bad, and she also realized her teachers were good people with good intentions. They cared about her and the other kids.

Her mother was more lenient with her. For example, she allowed her to watch a movie in the theater while she was shopping. They just agreed not to tell her dad. And the same held for taking the belly dancing classes she wanted. Again, her dad never knew.

When her dad laid down the law and forbade her from talking to her friends on the phone, she asked "Why" and was told simply "Because." He was the parent. She was simply supposed to obey.

That wasn't good enough.

She wanted an explanation for why she couldn't do things. There needed to be a reason. Her goddess mind was becoming stronger, and she wasn't going to shut it off.

She was hurt by her dad's lack of trust. There was no pleasing him. She started to assert her will, choosing to respond to his dominance with, "I'm going to do it anyway." Being a good girl hadn't made him trust her. So why bother? He still thought she was going to be bad. Why not live like she wanted to?

This bled into other areas quickly, like life patterns do. Her dad sent her to Catholic and private schools because she needed discipline. Again, she faced dominant teachers and school officials who tried to impose rules that made no sense to her without explaining their importance. For example, why did their uniform shirts have to be tucked in? Why did a non-tuck warrant detention? She thought it was stupid. She also wore patterned thermal tights—there was no rule about tights, so she pushed that line. What were they going to say, that she couldn't keep warm?

The men her age also seemed intent on telling her how to dress and what to do. She liked boys, so she'd date them—but also defy them. If they didn't like it, that was their problem. She was either out of there or they had to suck it up to have her.

Her rebellion turned into a string of personal and professional relationships where she hoped a male partner or boss would appreciate her, trust her, and love her/care about her for who she was. When they didn't act like this, she would respond, "Fuck you, I'm out of here." It was her dare for them to accept her—all of her. That was the part of her goddess nature that wasn't dead. But she was disappointed and hurt when they let her down or betrayed her.

She didn't really have female friends until her mid-thirties because she felt most of the women she encountered were living the formula her dad had tried to impose on her: be accomplished, get a good job, be married. She didn't want to be married. And she didn't feel the need to have the two kids and picket fence kind of life. Most women were assimilating around her. She was a fish out of water.

But then her goddess nature emerged big time. One day a long-time partner told her, "I don't want you anymore." They'd been having trouble and she'd sent him a letter voicing her concerns and feelings.

In that moment, she said it was like her goddess self sat down on the bed next to her. She helped my friend realize that it didn't matter how she looked, what she did, how much money she made, or how domestic she was. She could change everything to be this man's ideal, and it wouldn't make any difference. They would still be where they were. His feelings about not wanting her had nothing to do with her.

The act of voicing that truth freed her. She no longer needed to fight to prove she was worthy of love. She just was. She didn't need to struggle against anyone's perceptions of her or say fuck you to them when she didn't live up to their ideals. She stepped out of her prison, and she let go of the rebellion, exchanging that pattern for one of self-love. Goddess love.

ASSIMILATION

As we discussed earlier, others assimilate instead of rebelling. When a woman chooses assimilation, she decides to look, act, and mostly think like everyone else around her. She figures—mostly unconsciously—that there is safety in numbers. Standing out is too risky, she has learned, and it comes with a price.

She numbs out or silences the flashes of being unique, being special—her own goddess swagger. She wants to be like everyone else. She wants to be "normal," whatever normal is defined as by the group she's chosen to join. As part of this quest, she surrounds herself with women just like her.

She joins groups around shared interests because she's supposed to or because everyone else is doing it, even if she doesn't actually share the interest. She joins the local gardening club when she doesn't like to garden; the hospitality club when she's actually more of an introvert; the bridge club when she doesn't like to play cards.

People talk about cultural assimilation, but this is just as encompassing. It takes over the way a woman thinks, acts, and looks.

Unlike my BFF, I was never a rebel. Getting into trouble was a daily fear, and one I had to work for years to clear. Early on, I got punished frequently at home for questioning and defying, and those punishments were highly effective.

I started to go with the flow, people-please, and silence who I was and what I wanted. Part of the story I was living was this: there was no room for individuality in a family with six kids. Individuality wasn't rewarded at school or in church either. Questions were treated as dangerous business.

Soon I was walking the straight and narrow. I was living an identity composed of stereotypes: a so-called good girl—a good student, a good worker, the kind of girl a guy married but didn't fool around with, the kind of no-nonsense girl who got shit done and didn't ask for accolades. I chose friends and social groups based on these stereotypes.

I focused on working hard in my career of rebuilding warzones. I took care of my family. I was a good daughter, a good sister, a good friend (are we done with the stereotypes yet?). I was the one everyone came to when they had a problem, a crisis, or a major life transition.

And I wasn't sexy. Never wanted to be. I didn't make anyone uncomfortable with how I dressed. I never revealed too much skin. I made sure to consider other people's feelings and desires first and accommodate them.

My divine swagger wasn't just gone.

I didn't even remember I'd ever had any.

I remember one singular moment on a Friday night at a party I went to in Washington, D.C. Everyone had come in their work clothes, and since D.C. doesn't have casual Fridays because of Congress and other government agencies' dress codes, everyone was still dressed to the nines. The guys had on their suits and ties. Then there were the girls... They were all wearing business attire too, which included dresses with matching suit jackets, dress suits, and pantsuits like the one I had on.

At some moment during the party, time seemed to stop for me. It was like my inner goddess was holding the second hand to my internal clock, halting everything, so I could see what had happened to me.

As I looked around, I realized all of the women looked alike.

They all looked like me.

We were mostly wearing the same professional, understated clothes in neutral colors. Our hair was short, falling somewhere between the chin and shoulder. Our makeup was simple and understated, and so was our jewelry.

Everyone looked so much alike, I realized, there was no real way to tell any of us apart.

A part of me cringed in horror at the conformity. Like a shaft of light into a dark room, my goddess nature had reached me after years of dormancy. She'd broken out of the cage in which I'd left her, the one I'd walked away from and forgotten, and she was lovingly helping me remember that I was unique and special. That I wasn't made to look like everyone else.

I realized I didn't want to look like everyone else. I didn't want to become a blur in the crowd. I wanted to act and look and dress with verve. With swagger.

The experience shook me to the core—it woke me up big time—and I ended up leaving the party right afterward. I had to admit I'd assimilated. Conformity hadn't just invaded my life. It *was* my life. I was starting to look like every other working woman in D.C. who wanted to get ahead, be successful, and make a difference. It was like I was following a formula, and it wasn't a divine one.

I started to remember some of the events that had brought me into line over the years. One time a super powerful male colleague—someone I got along with and respected—shocked the crap out of me at a work retreat. Supposedly we could dress casually for this day-long retreat, and a younger woman in our office had done so. She'd dressed very feminine and looked lovely to my mind. But he turned to me and said, "She isn't going to get very far, dressed like that."

And then there were the ones targeted at me. A senior male colleague told me I could come along to the meeting with a major oil company if I wore "that black dress I'd worn on my birthday." My head spun when I read the email, and it took me a while to remember which dress he was talking about. My birthday had been eight months ago, you see. The funny thing was that it was a conservative black work dress. Sure, it was sleeveless, but I'd worn a jacket. That hadn't mattered to him. Even my deputy and friend at the time knew what dress this man was talking about when I mentioned it. Apparently I was sexy in it. Who knew?

I also remembered telling one of the junior women who worked for me that she basically needed to follow "the formula" like I had learned to do (something I've asked her goddess self to forgive). Remember how we talked about that in the last chapter? I shared how the men in our corporate unit were reacting to the way she dressed at work (feminine, pretty, sexy). They weren't listening to her in meetings. They were staring at her cleavage. I told her I'd gone through the same thing years ago. I was the only woman and non-military personnel at a peacekeeping conference, and some of the men mentioned to me after my presentation on black market activity in warzones (serious stuff, I thought) that all they could focus on was me and my sexy black boots as I walked around the stage looking pretty, well...hot. I was devastated at the time. But I took note.

I changed.

I had started to sacrifice my own individuality, my own femininity to succeed in a man's world. Except I finally had to admit that dressing more "conservatively" hadn't changed things. I still had male colleagues say things to me. I remember how upset I was to discover the senior managers had a pool going about what dress I would wear to the winter gala. I'd apparently caused a storm in what I had thought was, again, a conservative ball gown.

I'd followed the rules, and I was getting singled out for looking "sexy." Again! I just wanted to do my job well, be respected, and be successful. All of this women stuff was getting in the way, and it was uncomfortable to me. Changing hadn't made me invisible, which was what the shut down part of myself had wanted. I was still attracting attention.

That night at the party, my goddess nature started to unveil all the perversions of this formula I had been trying to make work for years. She was lovingly telling me assimilation was futile.

My goddess nature was always going to peek through.

Wasn't it time to let it shine through all the way?

I wasn't a mass organism. I was a beautiful, powerful, sexy, abundant goddess woman. There was no one else like me (or you, BTW, this is true of all of us goddess women) on the planet. When was I going to start think-ing and acting like her? When was I going to start expressing her?

Oh, shit. Here comes the change, right?

You guessed it. I started to press outside the so-called formula as much as I could in my personal and work situations. This wasn't a rebellion, though.

I wasn't acting out; I was reclaiming. My truest nature was surfacing.

Of course, when this type of reemergence happens, there are people who won't see it in a positive light. In some groups, no pressing of boundaries is permitted.

The thing is, we shouldn't have to worry about getting away with being a goddess woman. This is our purest form of being. Like we talk about in *Goddesses Cry and Say Motherfucker*, a key ingredient to our whole-ness as women is conscious expression—in all forms. Including our bodies, the vehi-cles of our goddess swagger.

You don't have to rebel or assimilate any-more. You can just be you. Let's clear any patterns of assimilation or rebellion you might have experienced or ones you still have going.

RECLAIMING PRACTICE #6:

Stopping the Stereotypes Invasion

Take a moment to breathe and let your goddess nature help you see what you need to about your life—like my BFF and I did. She will help you see whether you were a rebel or a follower.

How does it feel to realize this about yourself? Are you sad? Do you feel the urge to say, "FU?" Let's clear it all.

How about we start with you rebels? If you relate more to the "follower" camp but you had rebel moments, you might want to do this one too. Remember how I said I started to defy my parents and stopped after being punished enough? That was still rebellion.

All the ways I was a rebel, I transmute and clear them.

All the times I wanted to say "fuck you" to every-one and still do, I transmute and clear them.

All the times I dared the people around me to see me, love me, accept me—and all my reasons for doing so—I transmute and clear them.

All my disappointment for not getting what I wanted, for not getting more than I expected, I transmute and clear them.

All the times I got into trouble for rebelling, I transmute and clear them.

All the ways I hurt myself to spite them, I transmute and clear them.

All the ways I changed myself and my appearance to show them, I transmute and clear them.

All of the strategies I had—secrecy, sneaking around, not giving a shit, lashing out, etc.— I transmute and clear them.

How are you feeling? Take a breath. Your stories are going to surface. Let them. You can handle it.

I forgive myself for believing I had to rebel. That I had no other choice. That no one loved me enough to stop me, to tell me they cared.

Good job! You're doing great. Hang in there with me. What about the people who are part of your story? Do you want to let them go too? Maybe you hope freeing yourself from these stories will change your relationship, something we discussed in *Goddesses Don't Do Drama*. That's totally possible, but it doesn't impact your ability to delete the story between the two of you. It's their choice if they want to hold on to it, but you aren't participating anymore, regardless of their reaction. Make sense?

If you're ready, repeat after me:

X (Name), I release you from the role you played for me. Go in peace. All is forgiven and released.

I am me, and you are you. I have nothing to prove, and neither do you. This is done.

You might go through a few of the other people who have come to mind. You know the drill...

Are you back? Yay, you! I'm so happy for you. You're throwing out all of the junk that's been keeping you from feeling pretty and sexy and living in your goddess swagger.

Now we're ready to clear the assimilation junk. Again, if you've had any moments where you went along with things—even if you were more of a rebel—you might want to go through this practice to make sure you're all clear.

All the times I went along with what everyone else thought and did, becoming one of the crowd, I transmute and clear them.

All the places I sacrificed myself and my desires, I transmute and clear them.

All the reasons I felt I had to go along, I transmute and clear them.

All the people who told me I had to go along, I transmute and clear them.

All the times I hurt myself, I transmute and clear them.

All of the misery I felt in my silence, I transmute and clear it.

All the ways I didn't realize what I was doing,

I transmute and clear them.

All the times I acted in ways to make other people toe the line, I transmute and clear them.

How did your story get started? Why did you decide it was easier to assimilate and become one of the crowd? Let your goddess self show you. Let's take a moment and forgive ourselves for going down this road, if you're ready.

I forgive myself for believing this was the best way for me. I forgive myself for suppressing my goddess woman nature and being like everyone else. I forgive myself for believing this is what I had to do to receive love and be a woman.

Okay, take a breath. There's a lot of sadness here. I know how much sadness can emerge when we begin to see the choices that led us away from our goddess woman selves. The stories we believed, we *lived.* Just breathe and let it go. You've chosen to take a path back to yourself.

All the fears I have about being me as a woman and being seen, I transmute and clear them.

All of my worries that I won't be loved and

accepted, I transmute and clear them.

All of my fears about stepping out of line and wearing that dress and acting like...me, I transmute and clear them.

Everywhere I don't know how to be me, I transmute and clear them.

Everywhere I don't know where to start, I transmute and clear them.

If you feel vulnerable, it's okay. This is completely normal. You've lifted your veil and faced down the stories and patterns you've been playing out for years, and now you are free to start anew as the goddess woman you are.

Don't worry. Your goddess self has a plan for you, and it's perfect.

CHAPTER 5

OUR BODIES
ACROSS OUR LIFESPAN

We've worked on clearing all of the shut downs, stereotypes, and patterns we've accumulated that are keeping us from expressing and embodying our goddess swagger. Now, we're going to turn the stop-light on our bodies. That's right. Our bodies. 'Cuz we've got gobs of stories about them too. As we discussed earlier, there are so many different stories about what makes a woman sexy, pretty, beautiful, etc.

Let's face it. Our bodies go through tremendous transformations over the course of our lives. They are meant to...

And yet some things can't change. People are born with disabilities that make their bodies look different. Others, through illness or an accident, find themselves with a body that looks or functions differently than it once did.

If we tie our sense of identity to the way our bodies look at the expense of our hearts, of our happiness, we're going to be in for a world of hurt.

If we buy into media or cultural beliefs about what it means to be sexy, we're holding ourselves to a fixed standard that can't change with our bodies. What do I mean by that? If you believe X actress or model is the gold standard for beauty and sexiness, then you're judging yourself against her—for your whole life.

Let's talk average model stats. Some say a model needs to be around five foot seven and between ninety to one hundred twenty pounds while others say the ideal range is between five foot nine and six feet with a weight range of one hundred ten to one hundred thirty pounds. Most are young. Really young. They start out around fourteen or sixteen years of age and their careers are usually over by twenty-three.

Sure, there are exceptions, but these are the industry standards I easily came across while researching. Actresses might run slightly older, but even they discuss how the movie parts available to them change after a certain age. Sometimes they're cast as the mother of an actress who's less than a decade younger.

So what are we doing to ourselves?

As I write this, I'm forty-two. Do I really love myself so little that I'd try and look like a woman that I'm not and can't ever be? One whose age, height, and weight isn't mine? Sure, I can't change my height—unless I wear heels—but I could change my weight, right? Isn't that what we tell ourselves? It's in our control if we exercise enough, starve ourselves enough, puke enough. I can have the thighs of a sixteen-year-old model.

What about when we get pregnant? If you've experienced this body-altering process, then you know looking like some teeny, weensy model isn't possible during pregnancy, right? It isn't healthy, either.

Of course, the women we consider sexy

might shift depending on the time of our life. I can think of older actresses being discussed in that vein. Some pregnant women proudly show their baby bumps and celebrate their lush, fertile bodies. And we have plus-size models, don't we? They're helping to give us a new form to describe as sexy.

But we're still facing the problem: we're putting our conception of our own sexiness in the hands of another person. When I compare myself to someone else (anyone else) and find myself lacking, I'm falling into that trap. I'm not seeing the beauty and sexy in me anymore.

And this compulsion to compare and find ourselves lacking starts pretty young, doesn't it?

We need to clear our stories about what it means to be pretty, sexy, and beautiful at all ages and life stages in order to get back to our divine formula:

Goddess+Swagger=Sexy

Our bodies go through many different phases in life, and coming to terms with that—and accepting those changes without judgment or recrimination—will likely be an ongoing process. One thing I know for sure is that we are better prepared to handle any stories that come up if we love ourselves and have the tools to clear the hurt and anger and shame we might find ourselves experiencing. It doesn't matter how old you are right now. You can clear your preconceptions and stories about what beauty means at *all* stages of life. Think of the ages you haven't experienced yet as Goddess Prevention. Though clearing these stories completely will likely take some repetition, working on them now *will* make it easier to deal with these other stages of life as you reach them.

If you have a journal, you might want to grab it. Sometimes writing helps open up memories, thoughts, and feelings. We're going to read stories about other goddess women across the life spectrum. As we read about each stage of the journey, you can write your own stories too—either based on memory, for the parts you've already lived, or your feelings, worries, and expectations for those stages you have yet to reach. Or you can just visualize as we go along, using your goddess imagination. You can start clearing everything today.

Let's begin.

THE TODDLER

Madison loved to go to the grocery store with her mom. She especially liked sitting in the front part of the grocery cart and letting her mom push her through the store. Her mommy would hum while she picked up a carton of milk—Madison's favorite—and the chocolate chip ice cream. Madison would make gagging noises when the green beans and kale were added to the cart, making her mom laugh, which made Madison giggle too.

A woman smiled at them as Madison kicked her feet and laughed while her mommy tickled her bare legs. "You have a beautiful son," the woman said.

Her mom looked over, and her smile disappeared. "Thank you, but she's a girl."

The woman's eyes got big like Madison's daddy when he was playing monster with her. "Oh, I'm sorry. It's just...her hair.

I...never mind."

Madison lurched forward as her mommy gave the cart a hard push forward. "Don't listen to that lady, sweetheart. Your hair is fine."

While she didn't know why her mommy was so upset, she put her arms around her and hugged her. Her mommy hugged her back.

Every time they went to the store after that, her mommy always put a pink bow on Madison, saying "No one's going to think you're a boy." Madison tried to take it off because she didn't like it on her head, but her mommy always put it back on. Since her mommy smiled at her once the bow was on, she stopped fighting her.

She wanted Mommy to be happy.

The Young Girl

Nadia was so happy when her sister was born. She'd been waiting forever. Seriously, she was seven! All of her friends in second grade had brothers and sisters. Well, except her and Timothy Farnsworth, but his daddy had died and his mommy couldn't make babies by herself. Everyone knew you had to be married to make babies. And her parents had been married a long time. Like her daddy said, "They were due for a new baby."

Violet was so little when Nadia saw her for the first time. Her daddy had told her to be really quiet because the baby was sleeping. Nadia followed him into the hospital room as quietly as she could, walking on tiptoes like she did when she was playing hide and go seek with her mommy. No one ever heard her when she did that.

"Meet your baby sister, Violet, honey," her mommy said, smiling at her.

Nadia didn't know who to look at first. Mommy seemed tired, but she was so happy, happier even than when Daddy brought her flowers and danced with her in the kitchen. Nadia grinned at her, and then she looked at her sister.

"She's so little," she whispered, angling closer to the hospital bed. Her fingers weren't any longer than the toothpicks Daddy used after dinner. And her nose? It was little too. Nadia wished her sister would open her eyes so she could see what color they were. Were they brown like hers and Mommy's or blue like Daddy's?

Her grandma swept into the hospital room. "Finally! I have another grandchild.

Mavis, you took long enough. Goodness, let me see her."

Nadia edged over to her daddy and put her arm around his leg. Her grandma wasn't a nice lady. She pinched her cheeks and was always pulling on her clothes, saying things like "They just don't fit right" or "They don't look right on you."

Her mommy held out Violet, and her grandma tucked the baby against her body. "Well, you two did good with this one. She's going to be a looker. You can tell. And that hair. It's going to be beautiful. Just make sure you don't feed her all those sweets like Nadia or she'll get fat too."

Her daddy picked Nadia up and hugged her. "Candace, I told you not to say that."

"I'm only telling the truth," her grandma said.

Nadia felt tears well in her eyes as her daddy turned around and started walking to the hallway. She waited for her mommy to call her back into the room, but Mommy only had eyes for Violet.

She pressed her face into her daddy's shoulder and started to cry.

THE EARLY TEEN

Corinne just knew she was going to hate seventh grade. Aliens hadn't possessed her teachers, so they were still going to suck. The kids in her class still sucked too—except for her BFF, Janet. They'd met at middle school last year when they'd both moved to St. Louis for their dads' jobs.

Neither of them had known anyone. The teacher had made them stand up in front of the class and tell them something about themselves, so embarrassing, and they'd found each other afterward at lunch. Janet had grabbed a piece of pizza and said, "Didn't you just want to die when the teacher called you?" Corinne smiled for the first time since getting on the bus that morning. "Yes, it was awful!" They'd laughed and laughed about the whole stupid thing and become BFFs just like that.

Janet made friends easier than Corinne, but that was okay with her. She didn't need to be invited to everyone's birthday parties or slumber parties. Her parents didn't have money to buy them stupid presents anyway. And they could go to their dumb summer camp too. Except Janet had gone too since her parents *did* have money.

Corinne hadn't seen much of her over the summer, but they'd kept in touch, although not as much as Corinne had wanted. But today was the first day of school, and the only reason she was excited was seeing Janet.

When she got to school, she immediately looked down the hall for her BFF. Everyone was putting stuff away in their lockers, but Corinne could wait for all that. She spied Janet's signature Dutch braid trailing down her back with the rest of her blond hair. Corinne wished she could make her hair look like that, but it was short and frizzy in the humidity. It was like her hair was allergic to St. Louis' weather.

"Janet!" she called and raced through the crowd.

People gave her looks as she bumped into a few of them, mumbling, "Sorry."

Her BFF didn't turn around at first, so she shouted her name louder. This time her friend turned around, but she wasn't smiling like she usually did. In fact, she gave her a weird look.

"Hey!" she said, coming to a stop when she reached her. "I missed you."

Janet looked down, and Corinne knew something was wrong. Then she realized Tiffany and Stacy were standing next to her BFF. They were the most popular girls in the class. Everyone thought they were pretty, but Corinne just thought they were mean. She usually stayed out of their way because they'd made fun of her last year.

"God, someone got visited by the acne fairy this summer," Tiffany said in a dry tone.

"Or the pizza man," Stacy added.

Both girls laughed, and Corinne wanted to die. She knew her face was bad, but nothing seemed to help. Her mom said she'd had bad acne the year she was thirteen. It had only lasted a year, which gave Corinne hope, but it suddenly seemed like that year was going to feel like an eternity.

"Beats being a slut," she shot back, unable to stop herself.

"She's just jealous of our skin," Stacy said. "Come on, Janet. Let's go to first period and get away from this loser."

Corinne bit her lip, waiting to see what Janet would do. She lifted her shoulder, met Corinne's eyes, and then she turned away and walked off with Stacy and Tiffany.

The hurt welled up, and Corinne ran to the bathroom, locking herself in a stall so she could cry in private. She knew she was missing first period, but she didn't care. She'd lost her BFF, just like that. Janet had become a mean bitch over the summer. How had that happened? She'd been so nice last year...

She finally left the stall and went to the bathroom sink to wash her face. Her mom had said wearing makeup was only going to make her acne worse. As Corinne looked into the mirror, she realized it didn't matter. Even if she wore makeup, she'd still be ugly. Ugly enough for Janet to choose the pretty girls over her.

The Teenager

Addie was so happy when Robert asked her out on a date. She'd only gone out with a few boys, and nothing had turned serious. It was a little disappointing. She wanted to have a boyfriend like some of her friends. It would be nice to have someone to go to the movies with or walk around the mall together. And the kissing? She was excited about that, but she wanted to wait for some of the bigger stuff. Her mama always said, "Plenty of time for the serious stuff, Addie. Stick to kissing." And since her mama was always honest with her, she trusted her.

One of the boys she'd gone out with had kissed her, and it was okay. But not like she'd read about. Certainly not like in the movies. Her mama said it would feel that way when you met the boy who was the one for you.

Then she met Robert, and she figured *he* might be that one. Certainly he was cute with his green eyes and thick dark hair, and he played on the baseball team. She didn't like baseball much, but her friend Leslie had dragged her to a game. Robert had come up to them afterward. He and Leslie had gone to middle school together, and Leslie had done a little matchmaking.

When Robert came and picked her up for their date, she smiled as she settled back against the leather seats of his BMW. "Is this your car?" she asked.

"No," he said, pulling away from her house. "I have to get my grades up before my dad will fork out money for a car."

Addie wasn't sure what to make of that. She wanted to be with a smart guy. Her mama said that was the best thing about her daddy. A smart guy knew what he wanted in life and got it. Surely Robert's grades were good enough if he was playing baseball.

"I'm sure you'll get them up," she said.

He snickered. "I'm sure I'll get it up too."

She wasn't sure why he was laughing like

that, but she suddenly wasn't feeling excited anymore about their date. She made herself rally when he opened the door for her at the movie theater. The movie was great, so by the end she was feeling more herself.

"How about an ice cream?" he asked.

The summer night was warm even though she'd been cold in her sleeveless dress in the theater. "That would be great. I love ice cream."

"I thought so," he said.

Leslie must have said something to him. How sweet! He must really like her.

When they arrived, she ordered two scoops in a cup instead of a cone because she knew some guys got weird about girls licking their cones. A spoon was much smarter on their first date.

He asked if she wanted to go to the park nearby to eat the ice cream instead of hanging out in the parking lot. The ice cream parlor was packed.

She nodded. The weather was nice, and they could find a bench to sit on. When they got there, she ate her ice cream and asked him what he liked about playing baseball. He was so cute when he talked about it. She could listen to him all day even though some of the terms were unfamiliar. What in the heck was a butcher-boy single any-way? But she didn't want to interrupt him. He was talking excitedly, so much that he dribbled ice cream onto his shirt.

She immediately grabbed a napkin and started to clean it up. When he put his hand over hers and stopped it, she imme-diately stilled. Looking up into his eyes, she saw him gazing back at her, his eyes wrin-kled like he was thinking about something. Then he slowly lowered his head, and she knew he was going to kiss her. She real-ized she wanted him to. So she waited, her breathing becoming quicker. She hoped he couldn't hear it.

His mouth covered hers, and it was cold from the ice cream, which was a shock. He tasted like mint chocolate chip, and that was nice. She jolted in her seat when she felt his warm tongue press into her mouth, but she told herself to chill. It was only kissing. She settled closer to him and followed his lead, hoping she was doing it right. She opened her mouth wider and pressed her tongue back on his. Her heart was about ready to beat out of her chest, and her ice cream was freezing the spot it rested against in her lap. But this kiss was the best she'd had, and she wanted to savor it.

When he finally lifted his head, he was breathing hard. His eyes were shining. She smiled at him.

"Let's head to the car," he said.

She shook her head, looking around. He was right. They'd been kissing out in the open. Anyone might have seen them under the lamplight. Besides, it was getting late. She had to get up and go to church with her family in the morning.

"Thank you for such a nice time," she said when they reached the car after throwing their remaining ice cream away in the receptacle.

"It's not over yet," he responded, opening the car door for her.

She climbed inside and went to buckle herself in, but he stopped her as he settled into the driver's seat.

"I want another kiss," he whispered in the dark.

She did too. Kissing him was delicious. "Okay," she whispered back.

Their mouths met again, and she started to feel more confident the longer they kissed.

"You really are incredible," he said quietly, his hand turning her more toward him. "And you have the most amazing tits."

That startled her. No one had ever said that to her. Certainly no one had ever used that word to describe her breasts. "Ah… thank you."

His hand touched her breast and squeezed, and she pressed back against the passenger door.

"What's the matter, Addie?" he asked. "Hasn't anyone ever touched your tits?"

She shook her head.

"Seriously? When they're that big? Then I'm the lucky one because they're incredible. Come on, Addie. Let me touch them. It will feel good, I promise."

Kissing had felt good with him, so that would probably feel good too. She *was* curious, but this was their first date. "I…ah… don't feel comfortable doing that this time." She hoped that would soften the blow. She didn't want to hurt his feelings.

"Are you kidding me?" he said harshly. "You aren't going to put out?"

Her mouth dropped in shock. "How could you think that?"

"Because I'm doing you a favor," he responded. "You might have great tits, but you're a lard ass. Not a lot of guys are going to want to fuck you. You're lucky. I like big tits, and you have the biggest I've seen."

She crossed her arms over her chest, feeling the weight of them. Tears gathered in her eyes. She did have big breasts. F cups ran in the family. So did big butts. Her mom told her to be proud of them, but she knew how people stared at her body. She was only seventeen and she felt like a freak.

Clearly Robert felt the same.

"You don't need to do me any favors," she said, facing forward in her seat and looking straight ahead. "Please take me home."

"It's your loss," he said. "Trust me. You're going to wish you'd taken me up on my offer. With that ass, you'll probably be a virgin until you're forty."

Her lips started trembling, and she squeezed her eyes closed to stop the tears from flowing. She heard him start the car and prayed they would get home fast. All she wanted to do was go to bed and cry.

She left the car without saying anything, and he gunned it as he sped off.

Her parents met her at the door, and she started crying. They held her, but when they asked why she was so upset, she just said she'd had a horrible time. Her dad asked questions about him touching her, but she lied. She said he hadn't tried.

She finally ran upstairs.

In her room, she ripped off her shirt and undid her bra. She held it up, and the enormous size seemed to taunt her. Jiggling out of her jeans, she started to cry all over again.

She hated her body. She hated having big boobs and a big butt.

Robert was right.

No man was ever going to want her.

THE YOUNG WOMAN

Ellen was so excited when she moved into her new apartment complex. It had a pool! Sure, she wasn't excited about sharing it with other people, but she'd deal. It would be nice to cool off and swim. She hadn't had regular access to a pool since she was a kid.

She put on sunscreen before going to the pool so she wouldn't attract attention to herself. The wrap she wore covered her legs. Her childhood nickname, Chicken Legs, was still a sore spot. While she worked out and lifted leg weights, she still hadn't made them less skinny. Her small breasts could at least be enhanced with a padded bra. Thank God they had padded bras in swimsuits.

She walked past a pack of teenage boys and thought, *great*. When she took her wrap off and walked to the edge of the pool, she heard one of them snicker.

"Hey, it's a walking stick," someone said.

The boys laughed, and she felt her face flush with shame, knowing they were talking about her.

She slid under the water and tried to ignore them, but they were loud and rowdy. She continued to hear them even though she tried to focus on all the kids paddling and giggling around her, some of them wearing floaties and others balanced on brightly colored noodles.

"Whoa, check her out," one of the boys said.

"Man, she's hot," another boy said.

Ellen couldn't help it. She turned and looked. The woman who'd strutted proudly into the pool area looked to be about her age, but that's where all resemblance ended. She had on a yellow bikini, and her long, wavy hair was blowing in the wind as if even the wind had sped up at the sight of her. Her body was tanned and curvy in all the right places—in all the places Ellen wasn't.

The woman looked at her and smiled. God, she was even nice. Why did some people get everything? Ellen bet she had a perfect life. Certainly the rock on her finger indicated she was doing pretty well.

The boys watched as she rubbed sunscreen on her body and rolled onto her stomach, her perfectly toned and curved butt marking the lounge chair like a mountain might a beautiful valley.

Ellen felt the shame of her body all over again. She wasn't hot like that woman, and she never would be. She would never be that comfortable with her body. Boys had always made fun of her. Still did.

Why had she even bothered to come to the pool? Nothing ever changed. She was always going to fall short of other women—no matter how much she worked out—especially in a swimsuit. Who was she kidding? The hurt wasn't worth it.

She never used the swimming pool again.

The Pregnant Woman

Molly had always wanted to have kids, but she dreaded being pregnant. It was totally going to change her shape. She hated that. It seemed so unfair.

Her first few months were fine. It took a while for her baby bump to start showing, and when it did, she didn't mind it that much. Her husband, Henry, thought it was "kinda cute," and since she'd started to feel the baby move a little inside her, she was pretty psyched.

When her pants stopped fitting, she started to feel frustrated. She was going to have to buy fat clothes. She was only going to wear them for a few months, so it seemed like a total waste of money. And there weren't many maternity clothes she liked. They all made her feel like she was wearing a circus tent.

And then her boobs started to swell, and her bras didn't fit. Of course her husband loved her new boobs, but part of her wanted to smack him. What was wrong with her normal ones? Had he just been saying he loved them?

She started to dread having sex with Henry. Her body didn't feel like her. She didn't like it. How could he? He seemed glued to her breasts, and the baby bump got a lot more attention than her honey hole these days. Hormones sometimes helped, sure, but she didn't feel sexy anymore, and it killed her libido.

When she was nearly full-term, she finally had a meltdown. She looked in the mirror and all she could see was a big, fat person—not her. She hated being pregnant. Hated being fat. When Henry told her, "You look great, honey," she knew he was lying. By the end, she couldn't wait to get this baby out and get her shape back.

But after she had the baby and started working out again, she couldn't get her shape back to the way it had been before childbirth. And that pissed her off even more. She wasn't even sure having a baby was worth it if it ruined her body.

The Middle-Aged Woman

Betsy was patting herself on the back for being brave and going on her first date since her divorce was finalized. She'd signed up for a dating service to help tailor her options. It was time to put Derrick in the past—for good—and move forward with her life.

Most of the male profiles she'd been sent were for divorced men. That made her feel better. They would understand where she was coming from. Divorce sucked. She was glad her kids were in college, so it hadn't affected them as deeply. She'd gotten used to being a woman again and not only a mom—and then Derrick had gone and had an affair with his office assistant. It was embarrassing how cliché her life had become.

Before her date with Chris, she bought a new dress and lingerie and paid visits to both the hairdresser and the nail salon. Heck, she even had herself waxed. While she didn't plan on having sex with him, she wanted to feel sexy. Derrick had stripped that away from her by cheating—and with someone almost twenty years younger than her. The bastard.

That sore spot had led her to fudge a little about her age. She'd shaved off five years in her profile. She wasn't proud of it, but everything she read said men wanted younger women, even divorced men. She could always admit to the truth later. If a man cared about her, he'd understand and forgive her little white lie.

Being fifty and divorced sucked.

But she was getting out there, and that was more than some of her other divorced friends were doing. Some of them just hung out with women friends and kept busy with work, the gym, or volunteering.

When she reached the restaurant, she held her breath as she made her way to the bar. Chris had suggested they meet there and have a drink. She knew people started with a drink in case it didn't click. Why endure dinner? She liked the efficiency of it all.

She easily picked him out of the people hanging out at the bar. He was forty-eight and handsome, even if she could see a little age in the way his jaw had slackened. But he was a good dresser and well groomed, like he'd looked in his pictures online. They'd emailed back and forth before agreeing to meet, and she knew he liked going to art galleries, enjoying a strong Manhattan after a hard day at the office, and taking trips to exotic places like Bali and Seychelles. Since she'd always wanted to travel she was really excited about that possibility. Derrick had been too cheap and unadventurous to travel anywhere interesting.

Letting her breath out, she squared her shoulders and put a saunter into her walk, feeling the vibration of her heels on the hardwood floors crest up her calves.

"Chris?" she asked. "Hi, it's good to finally meet you."

He turned to face her, holding what looked like a Manhattan. "Betsy?" he asked. "I'm glad you found me. I felt a little buried back here in the corner."

His eyes fell to her face, and she could feel the scan. Some of the light dimmed from his eyes, but his smile stayed in place. She tried not to cringe. Could he tell she was fifty? Did she look older than her pictures? *Oh, God,* she thought.

"It's always easy to spot the handsomest man," she said with an extra-bright smile.

"That's sweet of you," he said and kissed her cheek. "Why don't you take my seat and let me buy you a drink?"

She appreciated the gallantry of the gesture and changed spots with him. She ordered a house wine even though she wanted to go for something stronger. Once she got through these first few minutes and settled down, she could go for a cocktail.

They started talking about easy things like their days and what they'd done over the weekend. She tried to put herself in the best light. Be positive. No man wanted to be with a downer. She also made sure to brush into him to let him know she found him attractive. She'd done her research.

He smiled at her as she talked, but it didn't seem to reach his eyes.

She decided to order a cocktail. It was the only way she was going to get through this.

Halfway into her Cosmopolitan, she noticed her date's gaze was wandering. Discreetly looking in the same direction, she caught sight of a beautiful woman, probably about thirty, in a strapless silver dress. She was drinking a glass of some blue concoction decorated with an orange peel. Exotic, Betsy thought. Suddenly her Cosmo felt cliché.

She felt cliché.

As she raised her drink, she was aware of the wrinkles on her hands and the way her arms seemed to sag.

Chris kept looking at the younger woman every once in a while as they chatted. Betsy knew he wasn't interested in her; he'd rather be out with the woman in the silver dress.

Chris was no different than her ex-husband. As soon as she finished her drink, she was going to lie and say she needed to head out. He'd understand. Like Derrick, he wanted a younger woman, a sexier woman, and she wasn't that anymore.

She'd sacrificed the best years of her life to Derrick—her youth, her prime—and she was never getting that back.

The Ill Woman

When Sheila learned she had breast cancer, she fought the shock and the fear. She was going to live. Somehow. She'd do whatever the doctors said. On her second visit, they advised her to have a double mastectomy. Phil held her hand while she cried, and she squeezed him hard when she saw him brush tears away.

They held each other in the car and cried, cried like they had after she'd had a miscarriage nearly thirty years ago.

"It's going to be okay, honey," he said. "You're strong. You're going to get through this. *We're* going to get through this."

She rubbed her face against his white dress shirt, praying. *But my breasts,* she wanted to say. They were going to take her breasts. How could she ever feel okay about that?

He gently pushed back and gazed into her eyes. "Sheila, I don't want you to ever think—not for one moment—that I won't love you or want you if you don't have your breasts anymore. Honey..." He broke down and started to cry, resting his forehead on her shoulder. "I just want you to be here. I don't care about the rest."

She broke down too because she believed him.

But after the surgery, she looked in the mirror at her body and cried. Her breasts were gone, the ones Phil used to caress and suck, the ones that had given her so much pleasure. Her babies had nursed from them. In their place was a wasteland dotted with wounds soon to become scars. She knew that her life was more important, but she couldn't help how she felt. She didn't feel like a woman anymore.

Then her hair started to fall out because of the chemo, and she experienced a new sense of desolation. Her beautiful hair was gone too. Sure, she could wear a wig, but it wasn't the same.

What was she becoming? She didn't have breasts anymore—or hair.

She didn't feel much like having sex either. The cancer was taking that away too. She secretly thought it was a mixed blessing. Phil didn't hold her the way he used to. He held her like he was afraid to break her, and given how thin she'd become, how fragile her body was looking, she appreciated his care for her. But how could he ever want her again—like she was now?

When the pain kept her up at night,

she wondered how she was going to face living as half a woman if she went into remission. The doctors had talked about reconstructive surgery, but it would never be the same. Her body would never be the same.

She didn't know how to feel about any of it.

THE ELDERLY WOMAN

Rosemary had never imagined she'd live to be eighty, and when she looked back, it felt like time had flown by. One minute she'd been marrying her sweet Charlie in her mother's lace dress with her twenty-inch waistline, and now she couldn't even squeeze her leg through that dress to celebrate their sixtieth anniversary.

Charlie didn't look like the man she'd married either. He was fat and bald and moved slowly, mostly because he barely got out of his chair.

She knew she wasn't a catch anymore either, but she wanted to look good for the anniversary party their kids were throwing for them. Their wedding reception was in the church hall—nothing fancy—but this party was at the country club. She wanted to look nice.

After Rosemary got dressed for the party, she headed over to the guest bathroom to put her makeup on. The light was better, and she could see any witch hairs she needed to pluck. Hopefully, she'd also be able to see any streaks from her foundation. Her vision had gotten worse, and her daughter had pointed out a few times lately that her makeup wasn't totally blended into her cheeks.

She took extra time putting her face on and spent even more time on her hair, teasing it up on the top where it was thinning, something that drove her crazy. But her shoulders slumped when she looked at herself in the mirror.

She didn't look beautiful anymore. She sure as hell wasn't sexy. No man had looked at her with any interest for at least fifteen years. Her sons told her she was still a catch, but they were sweet boys. She'd raised them to be.

When she walked out of the bathroom, she met Charlie in the hallway. He was wearing a nice blue suit and new dress shoes. His cologne carried to her, and it was pleasing. "You look good."

He grunted and walked past her. "I'll

warm up the car."

She stood there a moment. Tears welled in her eyes. He hadn't even looked at her.

She steeled herself. No one had told her getting old was nature's joke, and it was a cruel one. She hoped she wouldn't live much longer. Her body was just going to keep failing anyway.

How are you feeling after reading about all of those goddess women? We covered a lot of phases in life here, a lot of stories.

What stories came up for you? Is there one specifically that eroded your swagger?

Was a certain period in your life so far as a woman particularly challenging for you?

Going through these various phases and experiences is part of living in a body, though sometimes we can't predict which experiences will happen to us. Which will mark and change us most. Some women might not want to have children; some might want them and never have them. Some might never be seriously ill in their lifetime. Some might never experience violence or hunger.

The bottom line is that when we make looking a certain way one of the conditions to loving ourselves, we're falling into a trap.

We're also imprisoning ourselves, curtailing our happiness, if we don't believe there is something inherently beautiful or sexy about us—something that can't be taken away by physical changes.

We have to redefine our concept of what beautiful or sexy means when we face something new for us, something we discover we have judgment about.

Perhaps it's pregnancy, like it was for Molly. Maybe we have to contend with the judgments we have about our changing bodies in order to love ourselves and our pregnancy. When we have a hard time looking in the mirror and finding any beauty, maybe we have to ask our goddess selves to help us see what we cannot.

The most difficult time I've faced was when I was ill and almost died in my mid-twenties. Any of you who have ever been ill and had it change your body know how heart-wrenching this can be. I was supposed to be in the prime of my life as a woman, and yet suddenly I lost a ton of weight and looked unhealthy; one drug even turned my skin color yellow; I looked six months pregnant at times from the bloating in my belly from the illness. My hair lost its luster. So did my skin. And pain—the chronic, knife-cutting kind—ravaged my body and even the way I walked.

Of course people had interesting reactions to all this. Some didn't want to look at me, seeing something was wrong, while others stared. But a cousin's comment struck me the most. She said, "It's the best diet you've ever gone on." She had issues with her own weight; her comment only demonstrates how much of our judgments about other people stem from our own stories.

On top of everything else going on during a serious illness, the despair and depression that comes from us not feeling beautiful can ravage our spirit. I saw it with one of my best friends as she went through breast cancer much like Sheila did in our story.

These moments test the strength of our loving self-image. They test our ability to hold on to our goddess nature in the midst of these sometimes devastating physical changes.

Like in our goddess declaration, we have to be willing to look for the goddess woman in these situations, ones we are told are remiss of beauty, sexiness, and swagger.

As someone who has volunteered in hospice, I know there is beauty in people who are seriously ill, even those who are dying. The best way I can describe it is the light of their goddess selves still shines through. It might only be in their eyes or the curl of their lips as they try and smile at you through the pain or half-consciousness. But it's there.

I remember some of our hospice patients still asking someone to paint their toes or put lipstick on them. One even wore a purple hat she loved over her wig. They weren't going to give up their goddess woman selves, not even in the face of all that pain and suffering. I've been to war-zones and seen people ravaged by violence, food scarcity, and endemic poverty. People in these areas often don't sleep well, no surprise, and that takes its toll. Add in the shock, and their bodies are going through plenty of changes. Physically, they may not be healthy or strong.

And yet, they still stood tall and carried themselves with dignity; they still had swagger. Their clothes might have been dirty and torn, but they wore them with pride. I could see the beauty in them, especially the ones who had clearly not lost touch with their goddess woman selves.

All of this is to say we have goddess women walking around in all stages and situations on this earth of ours. We all need a little more compassion—for them and for ourselves. We're probably all going around with stories about our bodies unless we've cleared them and decided to love ourselves no matter what.

The body does change, but it's *your* body— yours to love, yours to enjoy, yours to bless, and yours to take care of. As goddess women we take what comes throughout our lives with love and acceptance. If we can't get to joy, we can at least get to peace.

In the end, no matter what condition your body is in, you are a divine being in that body.

A goddess.

We are all love at our cores, and that is the kind of beauty that doesn't fade or flicker. The kind of swagger you'll have as long as you're connected with your inner light. Are you ready to love your body in the now—across all your lifespan?

RECLAIMING PRACTICE #7:

Seeing the Goddess Woman in Every Stage

As we discussed earlier, you can clear any judgments you might have about the experiences or ages in our goddess stories even if you haven't gone through these stages of life yet. That's the amazing aspect about being a goddess woman.

Here's how I've been doing it. I've asked

my goddess self to reveal the judgments I have about becoming an elderly woman. That frees me from feeling and living any of those stories when I get to be elderly. Because I can decide how I want it to look and feel, you see.

Again, this might be a work in progress, but we're up to it because we're empowered with tools. And we love ourselves enough to keep sawing at the net that wants to snare us in hurtful stories.

Goddess women aren't bound by images of past selves either. We need to say good-bye to those past versions of ourselves with love so we can live in the now.

Let's start clearing.

All of the judgments and stories that came up as I read these stories, I transmute and clear them.

All of the ways I compare myself to another time in my life when I looked like X, I transmute and clear them.

All the times I've compared my body to someone else's, including my past self's, I transmute and clear them.

All the fears I have about a woman and her body as it grows up and gets older, I transmute and clear them. All my fears about getting old or sick, I transmute and clear them.

All my beliefs that I can't do anything to make myself more beautiful or sexier, I transmute and clear them.

All my beliefs that I won't ever be beautiful or sexy or have swagger, I transmute and clear them.

You know your story so far. You know how many life stages you've gone through and what you felt about your body in that time. Take a moment to think about a few of them. When you're ready, repeat after me:

I forgive myself for believing I wasn't pretty or sexy, for letting X make me think I wasn't pretty or sexy. I forgive myself for not seeing my true goddess self. I forgive myself for letting myself get this far without seeing it, without believing it.

Great job. You're choosing to connect more to your goddess woman self with every step we take here.

Are you ready to get even more personal?

CHAPTER 6

BODY IMAGE & SHAME

It's time to get naked.

Naked? Ava, are you crazy?

No. We need to strip down—metaphorically—and look at our naked bodies. We don't always have clothes on, and even when we do, we're aware of what's under them. We have all sorts of judgments about it too.

It's time to love your body all the way. The buck-naked way. I'll bet you have parts of your body that you have trouble loving. Come on. We're talking thighs, butts, bellies, arms, feet, breasts. I could go on, but you see where I'm going with this.

Body image issues arise pretty early in

young girls, according to everything we see and know about human development. Trying to live up to the media mania around being thin naturally leads to wanting thin legs, a small butt, a flat belly, small hips, and small thighs.

Bulimia and anorexia rates for young girls are staggering in the United States and certain countries in Asia and Europe, but even more gut-wrenching are the stats on how early these girls begin to hurt their bodies through vomiting or starvation. We're going to talk a lot more about this issue in *Goddesses Eat*, but it bears mentioning here. Hell, I even had a few pulls in that direction myself, but my goddess nature helped me realize it wasn't the way for me.

As we grow into our bodies, we start having experiences about body parts that often lead to shame, a major killer of all things goddess, sexy, beautiful, and swag.

I'm going to tell you a story about my breasts. You're going to have a story about one of your body parts, I imagine. My BFF had one about her nose. Another friend had one about her butt. I hear women talk all the time about a certain part of their body they struggle with. As you read my story, I want you to think about yours. You may even benefit from writing it down in order to clear it later.

I developed early, and in the fifth grade, I had the mortifying experience of having a teacher send home a note to my parents to buy me a bra. My mom had just had my brother, and my dad ended up being the one to take me. Totally mortifying, let me tell you! We were both so uncomfortable about it; I don't think we spoke the whole way to the store. He was dying on the inside too, I imagine. I sometimes ask myself, who thought this was a good idea?

I'm still grateful to the salesperson in the lingerie department for taking me back to a dressing room once she realized how awkward we both felt. If you've read *Goddesses Love Cock*, you know things like bodies and sexuality weren't discussed in my household in loving, openhearted ways.

Okay, so first body trauma. Check.

But they kept growing. When I was in sixth

grade, someone in my class started calling me BB (Big Boobs), and the nickname stuck for a while. Some girls were jealous of my breasts, and it still strikes me to this day how interesting it is that this kind of jealousy could exist in girls that young. Were they told they weren't as pretty or sexy if they didn't have breasts at an early age? As I mentioned earlier, the boys started trying to touch my breasts out of curiosity. This all led to me being very uncomfortable about this part of my body.

But the breast shame didn't stop. On a memorable car trip, my mom called my nipples Indian head nipples after the coin (they're large). This happened after my brother was discovered looking at nude photos of a famous actress online. Her nipples were like mine, you see. My mother said this—out loud—in front of my whole family (and that's seven people, folks)! Instead of taking it as a compliment—the actress was beautiful—I just remember the shame. Again, I thought something was wrong with my breasts. That my nipples were too large. My mom's weren't, and I was the eldest child, so it wasn't like I had a big sister around to tell me they were okay. I just knew someone

I loved had made fun of my breasts, much like the kids in my class had done.

When I was in college I studied in Spain, and for many reasons, that trip changed my life. Nudity was no big deal there. Let me say that a different way for those of you who need to hear it: the naked body was no big deal.

This was not how I was raised. Being naked was always huge. Your body was private, and no one should really see it. Heck, I don't remember being encouraged to even know what my body looked like. Certainly never to admire it as a thing of beauty. You were supposed to guard against showing too much skin, etc. Blah, blah, blah. Cue the stories...

In Spain, I remember how shocked I was to see a naked woman on a lotion commercial on TV *during the day*. There was nothing weird about it. My host mom didn't so much as gasp. I'd been taught women who posed naked only did so for things like girly magazines or X- or R-rated movies. There was always something sexual about it. Not here. There was no man leering at her. She wasn't trying to entice anyone. The point of the commercial was that she deserved to have this special lotion cover every part of her body because it was beautiful.

My world began to shift even more as time strolled on. Women in Spain went topless when they sunbathed as a matter of course, and there were more bare breasts than covered ones on the beaches. There was no shame around it. People didn't stare. It wasn't unsafe. It was just what they did. Blew my mind. I now realize I was also admiring these women's goddess swagger because they moved so freely in their bodies.

I wanted to be that free and confident in my own young goddess woman body. When I was alone in the apartment one day, I decided to sunbathe topless. It was a big moment and I congratulated myself on my bravery. The sun felt great, although I worried about getting sunburned in delicate places that had never seen sun.

I was feeling free and mature in my body.

Then I heard male laughter and jolted up. The first thing I saw when I opened my eyes were five young boys staring down from a balcony a few floors above me. And they were laughing. I immediately thought it was because I was so pale, and no one had nipples as big as mine. Cue the mortification again.

My goddess woman bubble burst, and I fled from the balcony with my hands covering my breasts.

A few weeks later, a friend invited me to the beach and made sure I knew it was a "come as you are" kind of beach, meaning you could be clothed or nude. Since I suspected I was going to be the palest girl on the beach—like I'd looked to those leering boys—and because I wasn't okay with having men look at me naked, I wore my swimsuit. I was also afraid of being laughed at again. Part of me didn't think I could handle that.

What happened on that beach altered my whole worldview. The people who were completely nude walked around like the woman in the lotion commercial. It was normal. No big deal. They had bodies. And they were swimming or sunning in those bodies. They were just doing it minus clothes.

Again, there was nothing sexual about any of it. Nothing felt weird or uncomfortable. I tried to imagine this sort of freedom at my community swimming pool back in the United States. It wasn't possible.

Even more important to my younger woman self was this simple fact: everyone's bodies were different. Some women had nipples like mine—whew, I was so relieved—while others had huge hips and small breasts. There were different shapes and sizes, and because there was no shame anywhere, they all looked so free. It was a smorgasbord of bodies.

It was also the first time I had seen that many male penises—uncut ones, even— and there were different shapes and sizes. Again, there was nothing weird about it. Women weren't leering at all these cocks bouncing in the surf like I knew they would have if this same scene had taken place in my hometown. Men weren't sizing each other up to see if they fell short, no pun intended.

Again, these people had swagger.

My Spanish friends joked with me while I was living overseas about Americans being so puritanical about things like nudity and the naked body, and in many ways, I realized that stereotype wasn't serving me. I decided to open myself up to other ways of looking at things like the body, sexuality, and sex.

It took me years to clear the shame I had around my breasts, but I got there. And the rest of my body? I'm mostly there. But I still have moments. And parts that my inner critic starts talking about. Sound familiar?

For example, the one that's been pulling me during the writing of this guide is that my belly isn't as flat as it used to be. Part of me—an unhealed part that doesn't think I'm as beautiful and sexy with a little belly because the media tells me so—looks in the mirror and wants it gone. Like it used to be. Like I know it can be.

I'm giving it too much energy, and it's on my mind a lot, meaning there's a part of me that thinks something about it is wrong and needs to be fixed.

Got any places on your body like this?

I'm on to the story and I'm clearing it whenever it comes up. I reaffirm that I love myself, no matter how I look. I put my hands on my belly and look in the mirror and say I accept myself as perfect right as I am in this moment. I'm in the process of acceptance, and I'll get to a place of peace about my belly. To where it doesn't matter what it looks like. It's beautiful and sexy—however it is.

Ready to look at your body?

Reclaiming Practice #8:

Loving Your Body

If you've been journaling while you're reading, this is another great moment to grab a pen and paper. Otherwise, follow along with your mind and heart. You goddess nature will help you find the best way for you. Let's clear a few things up front.

All the fear and discomfort I feel about facing my body, I transmute and delete it.

All the ways I don't want to talk about my body or be honest about how I feel about it, I transmute and delete them.

All the reasons thinking about my body makes me upset, I transmute and delete them.

All the reasons looking at or picturing my body makes me ashamed, scared, sad, or angry, I transmute and delete them.

All right, we just cleared some blocks keeping us from where we want and need to be. Now, I want you to think about your body. Picture it. All of it. Start with your face and hair and move on down to your shoulders and your breasts. How about your belly and hips? Look a little lower. What do you call the area between your legs? Do you shave or wax it?

Now, let's continue down to your inner thighs and your knees, calves, and feet.

How do you feel about all of it? If you're getting a little worked up or feeling resistance, just breathe through it. Ask it to be lifted from you. It's just unhealed parts of you afraid to remember your true goddess woman self and see her.

Let's take a scan of the back of your body, starting with the shape of your head, the nape of your neck, the curve of your spine, the slope of your butt, your cheeks. All right, ready to look a little further? How about the backs of your thighs and legs?

Are there any moles or stretch marks, scars, varicose veins, or freckles there? Do they bother you?

I want you to take the one part of your body that you've had a story with the longest. I told you the one about my breasts. Start with this part of your body; you can go through the other parts when you're ready. All right, take another breath. Has anyone ever ridiculed this part of you? What experiences led you to feel it was ugly or wrong or misshapen? What made you feel ashamed and want to cover up and not let anyone see?

Repeat after me:

All the stories I have around my X (Body Part), I transmute and delete them.

All the times I was made fun of for it, I transmute and delete them.

All the ways I think it's wrong or ugly or so not sexy, I transmute and delete them.

All the root causes and the people involved, I transmute and delete them.

All the reasons I can't love and accept my X (Body part), I transmute and delete them.

Whew! Take a breath, goddess woman. Feel like crying? Cry it out. Feeling angry and frustrated—like you're never going to love and accept this part of you, least of all feel it's beautiful or sexy? That's okay. This emotion has been trapped inside you for a long time now, and it's ready to leave.

All my hatred for my X (Body Part), I transmute and delete it.

All the reasons for that hatred, I transmute and delete it.

All my efforts to make it better, different, thinner,

perkier, toned, I transmute and delete them.

All the times I tried to change it and failed, I transmute and delete them.

Does this body part remind you of anyone in your family? Like the women in your family all have similarly shaped legs or the same butt, for example? Let's clear that too.

All the stories that this is what the women in my family look like, I transmute and delete them.

All the ways I don't want to look like someone else or have someone else's X (Body Part), I transmute and delete them.

How do you feel about this part when it comes to being with a romantic partner (either in the past or now)? Do you need to forgive them for some things they said to undermine your belief that you were sexy? Forgive yourself for believing them? Let's do it if you want to.

X (Name), I forgive you for saying things about my body that hurt me and made me doubt I was sexually attractive.

And I forgive myself for believing them.

If there are a few partners who really hurt you with their criticisms, you might take them one at a time. When you're ready, let's go back to this scene, back to your body. Again, please feel free to change the pronouns to best suit your personal experience.

Do you like your partner to see this part of you? Do you enjoy him touching and caressing it? Does he pay it any attention? Or is he part of the story you have about why it's not beautiful or sexy?

All my fears and beliefs that my partner doesn't like X (Body Part), I transmute and delete them.

All my doubts that he means it when he says X is beautiful or sexy, I transmute and delete them.

All the times he's ignored it, I transmute and delete them.

All the reasons I'm scared for him to see it or touch it, I transmute and delete them.

All the reasons I feel like I'm letting him down, I transmute and delete them.

All my fear that I'm not sexually attractive because of it, I transmute and delete it.

And if you don't have a romantic partner yet, do you believe this part of you is an impediment to you being with one? When you find that magical, wonderful someone, how do you feel about the thought of them seeing this part of you and touching it? How do you think they'll react? Will they love it and stroke it and enjoy it? Will you let them?

Let's clear anything coming up here so you don't take these stories into your romantic interactions or let them get in the way of a wonderful relationship and juicy sex life.

All my fears that he'll reject me because he doesn't like my X (Body Part), I transmute and delete them.

All the reasons I'm ashamed of it, I transmute and delete them.

All my fears that it makes me unattractive, I transmute and delete them.

All the stories I have around being with a man and him seeing my X (Body Part), I transmute and delete them.

Like we discussed in *Goddesses Love Cock*, loving our bodies is a key component to us experiencing pleasure in them, whether it be with a partner or with ourselves. The feelings we have about our bodies play into our sex lives (and even the pleasure we give ourselves—what I call Rainbow Time). Most of us also have a lot of feelings wrapped up in whether or not we feel sexually attractive to others.

Clearing the stories you have around your body and all of its parts is a huge starting point to loving yourself. This intentional reclaiming will unlock more and more of your natural goddess woman self, the one who is wired to be beautiful and sexy. When you believe that, you bring back your goddess swagger.

I've gone through all of the parts of my body that my inner critic has comments on, and I keep clearing any stories that pop up in the moment—like when I'm looking in the mirror after a shower or a bath and dressing. I can't encourage you enough to do the same.

When you love your body—and make a commitment to do so every moment—you change your whole life.

CHAPTER 7

DEFINING SEXY YOUR WAY

Are you ready to define sexy for you *all the way?*

Like we've been discussing, it isn't just about your body. It's about all of you. The whole package, the whole enchilada.

I've noticed that there's a common, catch-all phrase most people use to describe a woman they find sexy: there is just something unique about her.

Great news! You *are* unique. Like we discussed at the very beginning of this guide, you're hardwired for it. Every aspect of you adds up to something uniquely beautiful, uniquely you—you are love and joy encapsulated in a body perfectly designed for you and your life gifts.

Everyone knows that no two people look entirely alike, and that's what makes us special. Like the individual patterns of the tiniest snowflakes, our fingerprints are unique. So are our breasts, our hips, our thighs.

We were wired to be sexy!

This was my aha moment. And it's really great news. Take a breath and let it sink in for a moment.

If we're wired to be sexy, Ava, I know some of you are saying, why in the heck is it so difficult for many of us to believe? Sounds like the stories are creeping back in.

Let's review. This used to be hard (please notice the past tense here) because we got tangled up in outside perceptions and definitions about what it meant to be sexy and believed ourselves to be lacking in comparison.

We've even let the men in our lives tell us we aren't sexy. Well, they're messed up in the head too because many of them are buying into the same stories. Think about what guys might experience in this area:

girly mags, porn, lingerie catalogues, and fashion shows. So when our men look at us (if they're not living as their god man selves), they're looking for that story, that image.

All of it falls short of what makes a goddess woman sexy.

It's not about body type. It's not even about skin color. Or breast size. Or anything else, for that matter.

It's about *your* body—the one you were divinely gifted with—and how you choose to accept it, express it, celebrate it, and enjoy it. It's why little kids *love* to see photos of themselves or look at themselves in the mirror. They adore themselves. They still remember and believe they're perfectly made. They aren't sexy yet because they're still growing into their bodies, but they certainly know they're beautiful in their bodies.

But it's not just about the body, is it? Nope. The body is the vehicle, and yes, it has a form. One of my teachers used this beautiful phrase that really stuck with me:

*Let my inner beauty be reflected
in my physical self.*

We're talking about the special light we embody as goddess women when we're feeling love and joy, when we're overflowing with our own pleasure. Think about it. How many times have you heard people talk about a woman in love looking luminous? Isn't she told she looks great, perhaps years younger? Or the person having lots of sex at the start of a relationship? Don't people often comment, "Wow, whatever you're doing, keep doing it; you look incredible!"

And how many times have you heard someone tell a pregnant woman that she's glowing? Same thing. That woman is probably super psyched to be having a baby. She's filled with that incredible love and joy of knowing she's bringing another divine being in physical form into the world. She's going to be a rockstar mom and just can't wait to hold her baby.

That glow is the light of their divine nature shining through.

There is a physical byproduct to living your

goddess woman nature of love and joy. How we feel translates into this natural sexiness we exude from every cell. We don't have any blockages in our energy like the kind that develop from shame, anger, and depression. We don't allow the diamond we are to become covered in grime or mud from our stories or self-loathing behavior.

We live as goddess women, and we love every part of ourselves. Our divine radiance kicks into full gear, and it shows. Our skin is more luminous, our hair more lustrous. Our eyes are even brighter. Haven't you heard people say that?

We're happier. That also means we're less stressed. You don't have to be a doctor or a scientist to know that the body functions much easier—a.k.a. is healthier—when it's happy than when it's stressed.

How about we take a moment to really hone in on what it means, in practice, to be the sexy we were individually wired to be? Because this is all good in the abstract for some of us, right? How about a story?

A Personal Case Study

I've mentioned my BFF and soul sister before, but honestly, our goddess woman pairing is a fabulous case study.

We jokingly say she was born under a sexy star, and if you believe in astrology, her birth chart confirms it in spades. She's always been sexy. She doesn't question it. She doesn't even think about it. It's just something that has always been true. She told me recently that she feels the sexiest from the time she wakes up in bed until she sees herself in the mirror; that's when her goddess bubble starts to deflate from her stories.

Now, interestingly enough, she doesn't believe she's beautiful, but she's working on that part of her goddess woman self—like I'm working on believing and being sexy all the way.

Here's how her sexy plays out...

When we go out together, men frequently growl at her. Yes, you heard me correctly. Growl. The first time I was with her when this happened, we were walking in a major city during winter. She had on a nondescript black jacket, walking shoes, and jeans. Suddenly, a man walking toward us growled as he passed us. I knew he wasn't growling at me.

I was like, "Whoa, did that man just growl at you?"

Her response was nonplussed. "It happens a lot."

And she wasn't kidding. They do growl, but it's more than that. Men call out to her on the street, slow their cars down, stare, or fumble with whatever they're doing. *All the time.*

Like I said, she doesn't think she's beautiful, but there's something special about her, right? Let's dive in a little more.

Sure, she has gigantic breasts (and I mean F cups since I asked her if I could share the specs with you). She jokes that she couldn't hide her boobs even if she wanted to. A long time ago, she decided that if a guy was going to ogle her boobs, she wasn't going to be upset about it. They were a part of her, one she couldn't—and wouldn't—change. Basically, she wasn't going to take on the weight of whatever story the ogler(s) had about her.

Men tell her she has great legs, a great ass—even a great neck. I mean she's a magnet for compliments.

But she's also had her mother and other women tell her she needs a nose job, and that she's not as pretty as her younger sister. Even more interesting is that she's had some men say her breasts are too big; others have said they're too small. Again, she decided that was their opinion. Her breasts were what they were, and she wasn't going to feel bad about them because of someone else's opinions.

From my perspective, she's really good at knowing who she is and believing what she believes about herself. Part of this is the gift of that old rebel nature, right? She isn't going to let anyone tell her she's x, y, or z. Living as her goddess woman self, her old rebelliousness now translates to a greater inner loving and acceptance of who she is, what she looks like, and what her gifts are.

Trust me, she's got swagger too.

As I mentioned earlier, she's the one woman I know who's never felt unsafe in her body. Not once. She's now a martial arts master, but this goes back way before she became one. It was just never a shut down for her. In fact, when we went through the shut downs in these guides, she didn't have many. Her natural goddess woman sexiness stayed pretty much intact, not getting rewired or covered up through stories or personal experiences. And she was never really concerned about feeling like she needed to look a certain way or aspire to a model of beauty. She just was what she was, and she believed it to be great.

Then there's me... You've already heard some of my stories, so you know I never believed I was sexy. And I was never really told I was sexy. I mean, there were some men who had said it, but they were a part of the stories that held danger and violence, so it was all twisted and scary. I didn't want *them* to think I was sexy. I wanted them to leave me alone.

Okay, I had this friend imply I was sexy

once. Does this count? My dear friend in graduate school—a chief in the African country of Ghana—told me after seeing me throw a football that every man in his home village would want me for a wife because I had hips for birthing and could probably throw a spear. Are you laughing? Sounds like I was embodying his story about what was sexy. But it wasn't mine.

If I was told I was sexy in other rare situations, I usually believed the guy had an agenda—like he wanted to have sex with me. I thought it was a come-on, something he'd say to anyone.

Then I started calling back my sexy, my swagger.

But it looks different with me than it does with my BFF, and that's the point here. Every woman's swagger looks different. That isn't just okay. *It's how it's supposed to be.*

When I go out with my BFF, I'm sure some men think she's the sexier one. That's their story, and I don't take it on. She's not sexier per se. She's just *her* sexy—all the way. I'm uniquely sexy in my own way, and I'm continuing to clear ALL of my stories so I can embody my sexy all the way too. And I'm going to get there because I've decided to live like the divine rockstar I was made and born to be. We talk about how important the very act of deciding is in *Goddesses Decide* if you're interested.

Am I ever going to be growled at? I honestly don't know. Does it matter to me? Not one bit. Why? Because if a man growls, that's his story, not mine.

I feel sexy for me. I am sexy because I *am* me. I have my own goddess swagger.

I don't let someone else tell me who or what I am. They can confirm my thinking, sure, but their opinion won't sway me. And if it ever happens that I *do* let it sway me, I'll bring out my goddess tools and connect to my goddess woman self.

Do I believe looking like my BFF will make me sexier or give me more swagger? No. She's got her own thing going on, and so do I. Assimilating is a way to shut down our natural sexiness, not celebrate it.

I understand some women don't choose friends—either consciously or unconsciously—who are prettier or sexier than them, or have more swagger. Apparently there is a story going on here. You might check in and see if you have it running and clear it if you do.

These women don't want anyone taking the spotlight away from them, especially when it comes to men. In my early years, before I reconnected with my goddess nature, I remember rare but memorable pinches of jealousy or envy, thinking one of my friends was being admired more than I was by a guy at a party or a bar.

I didn't choose friends based on looks, at least not consciously, but moments cropped up. I remember being surprised when it would happen and being like, no, I don't want this kind of feeling in myself or between us. You're my friend.

I now have compassion for that part of my life and those relationships. You might need to look on them with love too if this pings a memory for you.

Because my BFF and I are living our lives as goddess women, we don't even think in these terms anymore. She is how she is, and she's awesome. I am how I am, and I'm awesome. We're just ourselves, and we love and honor and celebrate ourselves and each other when we're together.

Each goddess woman is sexy—in her own way, on her own terms—and has her own swagger.

Oh, and a little side note. Remember how I said my BFF was born under a sexy star? I realized this morning I can ask the Universe to add a sexy star to my sky too. Why do I know this? Because the Universe always rises to support our heart-felt wishes and desires. I figured, why not ask for what I want? You can too if you want one.

RECLAIMING PRACTICE #10:

Awakening to Your Beautiful, Sexy Goddess Woman Self

You know where you are right now. You know whether you believe you're pretty or beautiful or sexy or...well, none of the above.

This is your starting point.

Repeat after me:

I am willing to see everything that makes me beautiful and sexy right now.

I am willing to believe this about myself—maybe for the first time.

And I clear, transmute, and delete all the root causes and stories in the way.

Take a breath. I want you to pull up an image of yourself. It might be your favorite photograph of you or the time you caught a glimpse of yourself in a mirror and smiled. Your goddess nature is going to show you which one it is.

Look at her. Look at *you*. In all your glory.

Take a moment to look at every part from the tips of your toes to the top of your head. I know we did this before, but this time, you're going to see your body in a new light—a goddess woman light. Now close your eyes for a minute. Keep looking at her in your mind's eye and see the truth: the beauty, the lush, the sexy in every unique part of you.

Are you back from this beautiful exploration of your sexy goddess woman self? I highly encourage you to visit her over and over again until you can see her so clearly she's the only one you can see when you look into the mirror when you're brushing your teeth in the morning or getting ready for bed.

That's you!

Reacquaint yourself with her. Ask her what she wants from you. Because she might have some suggestions. There might be some places where you aren't living as your goddess woman self and believing you are one.

Your Goddess Woman Building Blocks

I want you to think of a woman you admire for being beautiful. Then I want you to think of one you admire that you think is sexy. These are women you feel like are really beautiful and sexy—and not living an image someone else told them to live. Maybe you know them personally; maybe you don't.

What is it about them that's so awesome? Take a moment to think about why you admire them so much. Is it their effortless sense of style? The way they saunter when they walk? The ease with which they handle the unexpected (situations, life events, etc.)? Their ability to take care of themselves? The pitch of their voice? The way they laugh? These are all elements of their divine swagger.

If you have a pen and paper, jot a few of these things down. If not, just hold the images and thoughts clearly in your mind.

Why is this important?

As you redefine what sexy is for you, you might need to see that what you want is possible in someone else first. Now, we're not talking about assimilating. This is not about trying to look like or be like someone else.

Let's take a deeper look at what I mean here.

I had one actress in particular I admired when I was first awakening this part of my goddess self. At first, I never imagined I could be as comfortable in my body as she was in hers. She seemed so sexy and confident. She had goddess swagger big-time. Then I came across a wonderful phrase:

Everything you admire in someone else already exists inside you.

I think I shouted a goddess woman *yes!* I was so excited.

There were building blocks inside me already. It was like my goddess self had kept them waiting for me all along. I was admiring things in someone else that I wanted to have for me.

I could work with that.

Still, in the beginning, I needed some ideas to try on. And this was another place where the people I admired helped me. For the first time in my life I had to ask myself what I really wanted for me.

That started with what I wanted to wear because I'd limited myself there with stories about what I thought I *should* wear to work or family events or personal outings (remember all the assimilation junk I had?).

I needed to seek out what my goddess nature craved to wear.

I needed to find ways I could dress that allowed me to feel both sexy and successful or respected—whatever stories I had going at the time.

And I had a lot of surprises... I discovered I didn't want to wear anything with buttons anymore. Too professional. I wanted bright colors. Soft fabrics. I wanted a lower neckline, something that accentuated my beautiful breasts—since I'd embraced them—instead of hiding them. I wanted to wear fun and unique jewelry, something I'd suppressed.

I allowed myself a goddess transformation.

It might be time for yours...

CHAPTER 8

THE GODDESS WOMAN TRANSFORMATION

Are you ready to transform completely into the fullest expression of your sexy goddess woman self? The one who has all the swag?

I want to be clear up front that your personal process of transformation does not undermine the importance of loving your body and its inherent perfection.

But like we've discussed, most of us haven't been really seeing our body through our goddess woman eyes, have we? We've had on shame-coated spectacles that see flaws everywhere.

Seeing yourself with your goddess woman eyes is step one of this goddess transformation.

The second step comes *after* you've started accepting the natural perfection of your body. You know you have the perfect hips or breasts or hair, but are you looking like your perfect, natural self? Or have you been covering her up? Most of us fall into the trap of being a rebel or a follower when confronted with society's expectations for us as women. In many cases this leads to our goddess women being covered up, concealed. This is where you ask yourself, *Am I dressing like I want and not how I think I must or how my friends do?*

Are you expressing yourself through your body without all of the stories?

Then you get to ask yourself what you truly want—with your goddess self's help—and make choices that transform you into your fullest goddess woman.

Let's get started.

Seeing the Lemons as Lemonade

As we saw in our stories, comparison is the biggest adversary to enjoying a loving self-image about our bodies and feeling sexy.

Any time we can't see the divine perfection in our bodies, we're comparing ourselves to someone or something else. It might be another woman we see out in the world, maybe even a friend, or perhaps it's someone on a magazine cover. Or it might be a version of our body at a different stage of life. When we weighed less, when our breasts were perkier, when our butt didn't sag. Fill in the story.

But it's a story, right?

Since we're goddess women, we're on to those shame-inducing stories. We admit them and clear that. No drama. No nonsense. We can bless the human part of us that still gets pulled into the comparison, the story. But we can also change our perspective. Instead of seeing something as a lemon, we can see it as lemonade.

Take my curly hair... I've accepted it. Love it. Embrace it. But it wasn't always that way. Way into my early thirties I wanted straight hair, the kind super models had that seemed to flow down their back in one straight, lustrous line.

I didn't think my hair was pretty. It exploded in humidity, and I lived in a place that had months of humid weather. I always thought I looked like I'd been attacked by wolves, and I used to even joke about it. Haha. That was me making fun of me.

I tried for decades to tame it. But it didn't matter if I put products on it. It boinked. And yes, that is a word I actually used. It never stayed in place. It never did what I wanted.

I spent tons of energy trying to make it what it wasn't. Spent money on products that didn't work, ones that piled up in my bathroom vanity cabinet. I was frustrated every time I looked in the mirror or saw a curl from the corner of my shame-bespectacled eyes.

I was in a constant state of self-criticism. And if I'm being honest, I was locked in a pattern of drama about my hair. And while *Goddesses Don't Do Drama* is about removing toxicity from our relationships, I can truthfully say goddesses don't do drama about their bodies either. This pattern of self-criticism and self-loathing is a form of toxicity too.

Haircuts didn't solve the problem. Neither did the weather. *I* was the problem. I had an ongoing fight with my hair—every day.

Do you have something like this going on in your life?

But this changed when I decided to live my life like a goddess woman. My goddess self had a list of things for me to address, parts of my body I was still trying to change, ones that were still skewed by stories and toxicity. No surprise, it turned out that my hair was on the Goddess Transformation List.

One day in meditation I felt my goddess self urging me to accept my curly hair, because it was a gift. It was what I had been given because it was perfectly made for me. I used my goddess tools and got there. My next task was to appreciate it. That took some doing, but then I also remembered other women—usually ones with thin or straight hair—say how much they envied my hair, like I had once envied theirs.

We were all locked in a state of comparison that was making us all feel lacking.

I asked my goddess woman self to show me the highest version of my hair; that's where the transformation comes in. I'd been seeing it as ugly and unmanageable for so long that I couldn't completely see the diamond in the rough (don't worry; we're going to do a reclaiming practice on this one). But I also knew I'd altered the natural perfection of my hair so much that I needed help to transform it back to its original sexy form. Think of it as an upgrade of sorts, the kind that brings back your highest version, the one that's always been available to you. Like I said, haircuts hadn't fixed my perception—probably because I kept giving the stylist pictures of actresses with hairstyles that weren't conducive to my curly hair.

I knew I needed some technical assistance; I couldn't cut my own hair. So I asked the Universe to lead me to a hair stylist who could be my goddess helper.

I needed a new, objective person who could see me, the goddess woman me. I was finally willing to see her. I was finally willing to allow my true beauty and sexiness to become manifest. If you read the Introduction shared by all *The Goddess Guides,* it won't surprise you to know this acceptance and appreciation came after my first full-moon encounter with my goddess woman nature.

I got that first haircut and I started to grow out my hair because I wanted to—something I'd never done. I had to clear a memory that came up in meditation where my mom cut my hair when my sister was born because it was easier for her to style that way. It's funny, but I remember her saying I had Shirley Temple-like curls before that; after she cut it—because she personally cut all our hair—it never curled like that again. Interesting, no?

I also had to let go of the story that professional women couldn't have long, sexy, curly hair and be successful. I've already talked about the Washington, D.C. look. You get the picture.

I started to brush my own hair just for the pleasure of it, something no one had ever done as an act of love. I did it for me, and I found it very soothing. Sensual even, I was surprised at first to discover.

Are you starting to understand the fullness of this goddess transformation process?

I basically loved, adored, and celebrated the miracle that was my hair. And I now feel it's a perfect facet of this beautiful, sexy woman I am—the one I'm seeing, the one I'm allowing every moment to express herself. Heck, I'll even say my hair has its own swagger. How's that for radical goddess thinking?

Sure, I still wish sometimes I hadn't started going gray at fifteen or had to start dying my hair at twenty. I still call in the possibility of my perfect original hair color returning because I'm a goddess woman. I can ask for something I want, something that was mine, to be restored to me. But I'm not attached to it. Do I dye my hair? Yes. I'm not taking on a story about that altering my natural perfection. I do it because it's my choice. Maybe that will change, and I'll stop. I allow my goddess self to guide me. She's the master transformer.

How do you feel about adoring yourself? Your body? Is there a part of you that your goddess self wants you to see differently?

Is there something she wants to help you upgrade?

Reclaiming Practice #11:

Polishing the Diamond

We already took a huge step toward loving and accepting our bodies and all of the body parts we have trouble seeing as beautiful and sexy.

Now we're going to make a list of the parts of ourselves our goddess woman selves want us to transform, to restore. Pick one to start with for our purposes here (like I did with my hair). Have the intention of going through the other items on your list one at a time, giving each the attention it deserves. Maybe you don't feel ready to take on X yet. That's okay too.

The right time and sequence is yours to discover with your goddess woman self, and yours to choose. She won't ever force you to do anything you don't want or to act too fast. It's always your choice. She's just your friendly guide, or as I like to call her, your best friend.

Do you have your item? Repeat after me:

All of the reasons I've been blocked, resistant to, or afraid to allow X to become its highest version, I transmute and delete them.

All my disbelief that X can be beautiful, sexy, pretty, or appealing, I transmute and delete it.

All the blocks keeping me from imagining this could ever happen, I transmute and delete them.

All of the reasons X hasn't been the diamond my goddess nature knows it to be, that it was born to be, I transmute and delete them.

I allow X to be polished up and revealed as the diamond it truly is.

And all the stories about how I should cover it up (whether from me or from someone else), I transmute and delete them.

I am free to be me, to transform and upgrade X. I am a beautiful and sexy goddess woman at a whole new level—starting right now. I am the goddess woman I was designed to be.

I adore X and the rest of myself.

I allow new people to show up to help me uncover my goddess woman. I allow miracles and magical meetings to happen. It doesn't have to cost a lot of money or take a lot of time. But it also can if I want it to. Either way, I'm worth it.

I promise to get out of the way and let it unfold naturally.

Congratulations, goddess woman! You just transformed yourself.

Ready for more?

Oh yeah, you're ready.

MAKING GODDESS WOMAN CHOICES

It's time for step three of this transformation process. This is where you make sure you're choosing what works for your goddess woman, what resonates with your unique sexy nature, your swag. If you aren't, your goddess self is going to ask you to trust her to help you start doing so.

Maybe you've been dressing defensively

like I did; I didn't wear dresses and skirts for a long time because I was afraid it would make it easier for a man to assault me. I had the thought I might be able to get away easier. That's how unsafe I felt in my body.

But here's the thing. I really wanted to wear dresses and skirts. I even envied women who wore them so easily and comfortably.

Perhaps you've been covering up your goddess woman self out of shame. I'm thinking of the women I know who cover their faces up with long hair or wear baggy clothes so they can hide or won't be seen.

Or maybe you've been dressing to impress. I'm remembering an old friend and colleague who sought esteem by being a member of elite women's groups and professional organizations. She wore very expensive and tailored attire when she would have preferred jeans and a T-shirt.

If you've been choosing what you wear and how you look out of rebellion or assimilation, you've also been covering up your true goddess woman self's swagger.

Are you ready for your transformation to keep rolling?

Remember how I mentioned the list your goddess self has for you? Well, here's how more of my transformation process unfolded.

When I started to express my individuality—to reclaim my femininity—I had to pick and choose where I could wear my new things. At my old work in Washington, D.C., there were small changes. I might wear a bright-colored silk scarf with a brown pantsuit. The tan heels I wore might have a leather crisscross pattern that made them look less plain. I wore some of the necklaces I'd bought in foreign countries because I felt that if it was tied to work, I could get away with it.

Like we've already discussed, I started to grow my hair out. In the beginning, I'd wear it up at work.

The sad fact was: I was still afraid I couldn't express my newly emerging goddess self in that corporate workplace without being penalized for it.

But in my personal time at home, I could let my full goddess nature fly. As I mentioned earlier, I started to explore new kinds of clothes. Ones without buttons and collars. Ones that didn't need dry cleaning. Comfortable ones that had a sensual feel on my newly sensitized skin—a gift from my goddess woman body since before I had been completely disconnected from my body out of shame and fear.

Again, since I had cleared the old stories around my breasts, my goddess self encouraged lower necklines over the ones I'd had cinching around my neck. I even bought new bras with matching panties because it made me happy to honor them with something special.

I bought new skirts that swished when I twirled because Ginger Rogers had always made that look fun. I paid attention to the "fun" feeling. It was a wonderful guide during my transformation—let it be a guide for you too.

And if some of you are worrying this is going to cost a lot of money, that wasn't the case for me. We're also going to talk about feelings of scarcity and self-worth around money in *Goddesses Deserve The Gs* in case you're interested.

Allow the Universe to serve you up the perfect transformation at a price you're comfortable with. If you don't have much in the way of funds, you might find things on sale. A friend might give you the perfect dress they no longer wear or one they've never even worn.

But you might also find that part of your journey is to finally decide you deserve to spend some money on things that make your goddess woman self happy—on your-self—and to let go of the stories that keep you from buying something.

I let my goddess nature guide me to all of it—colors that made me smile, made me light up, made me *want* to wear them. I also took inventory of the clothes I had, only to reel in horror from the realization that I had fifteen pairs of black dress pants—all in different styles. I started to give these clothes away to make room in my closet for my new goddess collection.

I remember wearing one of my beautiful new dresses to my parents' home for Christmas. It was a rich garnet color, and it gathered around the bust and then fell in a loose shape to mid-calf. I had tights on, but at that time, I was aware the dress was shorter than the clothes they were used to seeing me wear. The moment I walked into the kitchen, my dad's eyes zeroed in on me and then immediately dropped to my hemline.

I was in my mid to late thirties at the time, and I still cringed at the judgment emanating from him. The other part of me was like, "Seriously? Are we still here?"

The first time I wore a bikini at my parents' house, not too many months later, I ended up crying in the bathroom because that step was so hard for me. It was a beautiful green one, and I loved how I looked in it. Wearing it was me saying that I wasn't going to cower in shame anymore. I was going to celebrate that I had a body, a goddess body.

My goddess choices were part of my own process of transformation, and they empowered me with all the healing I needed to uncover her again.

And I had to go through this process with everyone around me because this woman was completely new (foreign even, in some cases) to them. Some of them were cool with the new me. Some of them were comfortable seeing my goddess woman's sexy emerge at higher levels. Some weren't.

But I wasn't going to let their stories or judgments (and mine) deter my goddess woman self from transforming. This is something we talk a lot about in *Goddesses Don't Do Drama* and *Goddesses Cry and Say Motherfucker* if you want an extra goddess woman boost in this department.

The process of transformation continues throughout our lifespan as we grow as goddess women. Now, years after this first goddess transformation, I know what I want to wear and how I want to look. I continue to let my goddess woman swagger emerge and grow. I keep allowing my goddess self to guide me, but I also trust myself more than ever before.

I also know what makes me happy, and having back my sexy and my swag makes me happy. Euphoric. Joyous. That's the ding-ding-ding when you're going through this process.

If you remember one thing from reading *The Goddess Guides to Being a Woman*, remember this simple truth: You can't fake joy.

You can fake love—you can lie to yourself about it, either because you don't know how it should feel or because you think what you have is all you can get. You can even fake pleasure. But you cannot fake joy.

It's impossible. Let that be your bellwether. It can never steer you wrong.

So how does one start this personal goddess transformation? Here are some of the actions you can take:

- Write down the things your goddess self has for you to transform
- Take the list of characteristics about the beautiful and sexy woman you admire (like confidence, honesty, or free-

dom of movement) and start applying them to yourself or ask your goddess self to help you see how to do it

- Create a vision board of hairstyles, clothes, and accessories that make you happy and start looking for them in the world (you will find them, trust me)
- Buy the clothes, shoes, accessories you want—even if you don't feel you could ever wear them (in one case, it took me two years to feel brave/confident enough to wear this super sexy dress I wanted)
- Make a list of what makes you feel beautiful and sexy and surround your-self with those things or, in the case of activities, do more of them on a daily/weekly/monthly basis
- Call in new goddess women helpers like new stylists, salespeople, etc. to help your goddess woman self emerge even more (I even ran into a makeup artist on one occasion who gave me a divine consult for free and helped me see how to apply mascara that worked with the natural shape of my eyes. I'd copied someone else's style here, and it was obscuring my diamond)

- Pay attention to how you move in different situations (like when you walk into a restaurant or see other men or women noticing you on the street). Are you moving freely or comfortably? Are there stories you need to clear? Then play with the feeling in your body to unlock your natural goddess walk
- Keep a journal about any insights you have, like the stories and fears you might have about being sexy and having swagger. Blast them out, and take note of how different you start feeling about yourself, the real you
- Listen to your intuition (like if it's asking you to consider reverting to your natural hair color and not bleach your beautiful brown hair)
- Take a Relationship Inventory like we discussed in Goddesses Don't Do Drama and make sure you are surrounding yourself with men and women who support you expressing you as a sexy goddess woman with swagger

This is a process that, as discussed, continues over your lifespan. The more you get to know your goddess self, the more second-nature your choices will become. But it's not all about the clothes or the hair or about the body...

We are sexy and have swag in our purest essence.

RECLAIMING PRACTICE #12:

Bring Back the Sexy Woman in the Sheets

We've talked about getting naked before, but we needed to discuss a few more items about our bodies and clear some more stories before we were all ready for this practice.

For many of us it's a humdinger. It came to me in meditation how important it was to include this reclaiming practice (even before my BFF told me this was when she felt the sexiest). I'll be honest though. Part of me was like, seriously? I'm going to reclaim that? Me? That was my story rising up to entangle me.

But it all made sense too. While writing this guide, I discussed what it means to be sexy with the men in my inner circle, and one of the things they said grabbed my goddess woman's attention. They said there was nothing sexier than seeing the woman they cared about or loved in the sheets—no makeup, no perfect hair.

Remember how I said we're wired to be sexy? This common agreement from the men I know confirms it.

It's time to bring back that sexy woman in the sheets. In case you're still processing this, I mean *you*.

Because it's us stripped down of all the so-called conventions of what it means to be sexy (clothes, makeup, shoes, etc.).

I'll even go out on a limb and say that sex doesn't need to have anything to do with this. We can look sexy in a sheet even if no one's there; my BFF feels this way. Why? Because we're sexy just 'cause. Not because we're with someone. Let's put it this way, it's you feeling so juicy and wonderful in your goddess woman skin and self that no one else needs to tell you how sexy you are. You just know it.

Some of you may sleep nude already; it took me six months to feel comfortable doing so, but I knew it was what my goddess woman self wanted me to do. I felt like I was choking in my nightgowns, and I realized I had a ton of stories related to why I was afraid to sleep nude. Most of it had to do with not feeling safe or comfortable in my body.

Whatever you sleep in or don't sleep in doesn't matter. I'll bet you've been naked in bed at least once if you've ever had sex. Work with that. If you haven't ever been naked in bed, I want you to imagine it. I'll bet you're going to have all sorts of stories come up, and you can use your goddess tools on them if you want to.

We're just going to go through this exercise using our imaginations; if you're already reading this naked in bed, awesome. If you want to get naked in bed later, awesome. Do whatever you are called to do.

Our purpose is to clear any of the blocks you may have to believing you are sexy all stripped down. No accessories. No clothes. *Nada.* Only your sexy, beautiful goddess woman body. Ready? Take a breath.

I want you to picture yourself alone in bed. Naked. I want you to feel the sensation of your body brushing against the sheets. Is your skin sensitive? Does it feel delicious or uncomfortable?

There's no makeup on your face, and who knows what your hair looks like. It doesn't matter. You don't even think about it. You don't care.

You know you're a goddess woman and your body is freakin' gorgeous. It was perfectly made for you to enjoy and feel pleasure in. Right now, you're feeling pleasure in being nude with the top sheet barely covering you. Maybe your leg is peeking out. Maybe one of your breasts is.

You revel in this moment, in your body.

Got it?

Let's clear any stories coming up that block you from feeling sexy right now.

All the ways I'm scared of my own body, of being naked, I transmute, delete, and clear them.

All of the reasons this practice is so hard for me, I transmute, delete, and clear them.

All of the reasons I can't believe I'm sexy just like this, without makeup or styled hair, I transmute, delete, and clear them.

If none of my lovers have ever told me I was sexy when they woke up with me, I transmute, delete, and clear my disappointment and the stories this has given me.

The stories I carry about how this seems silly or crazy or a little slutty, I transmute, delete, and clear them.

All my embarrassment about doing this exercise—and my fear about seeing myself this way (even in my mind's eye)—I transmute, delete, and clear it.

All of the reasons I want to shut this off, shut this down right now, I transmute, delete, and clear them.

All my beliefs that my body couldn't be this sexy, I transmute, delete, and clear them.

The stories I've internalized that this only happens in the movies, or it only works for models or actresses, I transmute, delete, and clear them.

All my feelings that this is wrong and bad and sinful, I transmute, delete, and clear them.

Take a deep breath. Take another. There is a lot of energy here. Lots of stories.

Remember how we've talked about reacquainting yourself with your goddess woman self and looking for her in the mirror. You might look for her here too. If you meditate, you might visualize this practice and see what happens. I know your goddess self would be cheering you on.

Feeling comfortable in our bodies—free of any clothing or makeup—is a precious gift.

Reclaiming Practice #13:

Letting Out Your Sexy, Your Swag

Does all of this feel a little overwhelming? Don't worry. You can take it at your own pace. It took me a few years to go through my major goddess transformation. Hair doesn't grow out overnight, does it? The biggest thing is starting, taking that first step.

How about we clear all the stories keeping you from letting out your full sexy, your full beautiful right now? It's time.

The feeling that this is all too daunting, I transmute, delete, and clear it.

All of the reasons I don't think I can do it, I transmute, delete, and clear them.

All my disbelief that I can never be fully sexy or completely beautiful, I transmute, delete, and clear it.

All my stories about how a process like this doesn't work for me, and my memories of "makeovers" that haven't worked before, I transmute, delete, and clear them.

All my beliefs that it will cost too much money or take too much time to be worth it, I transmute, delete, and clear them.

All my fears of what people might think—especially X (Name)—I transmute, delete, and clear them.

All my doubts about my ability to do this or have swagger, I transmute, delete, and clear them.

All my blocks from hearing this goddess self of mine talking to me, I transmute, delete, and clear them.

All my hesitancy to upset the apple cart of my life by being sexy or beautiful, I transmute, delete, and clear it.

All my fears that it will change nothing, I transmute, delete, and clear them.

All my fears that it will change everything, including the things I do not want to change and those that I do, I transmute, delete, and clear them.

All the reasons I think this is great for other women, but not me, I transmute, delete, and clear them.

All the reasons I believe I'll never really be a goddess woman with swagger, I transmute, delete, and clear them.

Whoa! There were still some stories inside you, weren't there? Don't worry. It's all unfolding perfectly—perfectly for you.

Okay, now let's bring this all together.

Swagger Your Way: Living as a Divine Rockstar

It's time for the Big Blend.

We've called out the junk keeping us from seeing we're wired to be sexy and started clearing it; this is going to be process. We've started redefining sexy for ourselves and created some action items for how we can start fully expressing ourselves as goddess women in our bodies.

Now we're going to blend it all together to complete our divine formula at the highest level possible.

Hello, goddess swagger.

Now that you've chosen to love all of you, you're ready to start seeing yourself as a

divine rockstar, one who has unique swagger. It's time to believe it. And express it.
Fully.

You are a divine rockstar, a goddess woman
with a swagger all her own.

Let's break it down... Because I know you
are still getting used to this term, this idea,
this new way of being.

As women we aren't really taught we have
swagger, are we?

In fact, we're taught pretty quickly that
there's a fine line between arrogance and
confidence. You know the stories; we
covered a lot of them earlier in our soul-
leeching stereotypes. A woman who toots
her own horn and is assertive is often considered a bitch. A woman who thinks she's
special isn't being humble. There are a
million ways we're told not to have swagger, and it stems from stories about what it
means to be a good girl, a good woman, a
good wife, a good mother, a good worker,
etc.

Men, however, are encouraged to find

their swagger, whether or not it's explicitly called that. They're encouraged to speak their minds; handle themselves; excel and be admired for it (can we say athletes anyone?); ask for what they want, go after it, or take it; talk about their accomplishments. And this is just a tiny list of what supposedly makes up a successful, confident man.

Whatever you think of rap, there is a predominant masculine story present, one I was guided to closely examine to help us. Some of you might think I'm crazy right now (and that's a story), but there are some important divine truths in rap about swagger and expressing our fullest selves in our bodies, ones for us to glean as goddess women.

These men believe—or claim to—that they are "the shit." They walk into a room fueled by the belief they have a big enough cock (or whatever the line is), because most men feel this is important to their perception of themselves. A man with a big cock is perceived as strong and successful. It commands respect, and if you've ever heard men talk about standing next to other men at the urinals in the men's bathroom, you know what I mean. (Side note: We're *all* told body stories.)

These men have people wanting to be around them, women especially, because they're special or unique. Other men respect them and what they do, how they roll. They bring in the money, and they live life on their own terms. When haters try and dull or stop their swagger, they say, "Fuck 'em" or they ignore them. They know it's the other person's problem. Not theirs. And they won't stop being who they are because of the critics.

Sound familiar? That's divine rockstar energy, folks. You can take out the parts that don't work for you about rap, especially the lyrics about women and so on (whatever your stories are here). But these men are on to something. They seem to remember part of their divine nature and have given themselves permission to have swag. You might even say they are encouraged to have it and rewarded for it. That they became rap gods and legends because of it.

Well, we're all gods and goddesses in a

body, so we have the one part down.

The thing is, women aren't told they can have swag. We aren't really even taught what it is, what it would look like for us.

It's like this part of the divine formula was secreted away from us. We all know how women's sexuality was seen as a threat across the ages; how religious, social, and political institutions sought to—and still seek to in some places—control a woman's sexuality and her expression of it (dress, comportment, etc.), her ability to have a purpose outside of the home. These are all components of her swag (because it's not just about sexuality or a career) in addition to the unique gifts she was born with.

So, how does goddess swagger look in action?

One woman drinks a cup of coffee with her legs crossed because it's her way; another woman walks with a saunter that accentuates her curvy hips because she's in sync with the way her body wants to move; another woman unconsciously tucks her hair over her shoulder when she's reading;

another laughs loud and gusty when something has tickled her goddess woman self; another woman looks across the room at someone without saying a word.

Swagger can be quiet or loud, understated or bold. It depends on how your goddess woman chooses to express herself. The point is to express, and the way we express ourselves in this body is our swagger. And our swag should be ours to express, to play with, to create with.

If you've lost it—the precious connection to your divine rockstar and the swagger that comes with it—we're going to bring it back.

Let's talk about the elements of swagger one last time so it can all sink in at the highest level for you:

- Acceptance and expression of the uniqueness of your body, the way you move, the way you talk—all of it
- Self-appreciation, adoring even, of your uniqueness
- Love for everything you are as a goddess woman

- Confidence in who you are and the choices you make
- Trust in yourself
- The willingness to be seen in the world as a goddess woman
- The willingness to enjoy being in the body
- The willingness to experience pleasure in the body (and not just the sexual kind, all kinds)
- The willingness to be sexually appealing
- The willingness to be loved and admired for who you are and what you give to the world by being you

Are you ready to see how this unfolds in your divine rockstar life? Are you ready to let your goddess woman self take you the rest of the way?

Chapter 10

Goddess Declaration: The Divine Rockstar

That's right. It's time to say it. Out loud if you really want it to pack a punch.

Repeat after me:

I, Name, hereby agree to be sexy, to allow my goddess swagger to come back all the way. I am beautiful. I am sexy. I do have swagger, my own swagger.

No one is beautiful or sexy like I am. No one has swagger like mine. No one can do what I can do in the world.

I am unique.

I am perfect.

I am a goddess woman.

I am a divine rockstar.

Damn skippy you are!

Don't let anyone tell you otherwise.

Until we meet again, goddess woman.

Get your swag on.

General Tools for Connecting to Your Goddess Nature

While each of *The Goddess Guides* is focused on a specific topic, there are some general tools I wanted to pass along that I've found helpful for getting in touch with one's goddess nature. I'm sharing this chapter—like the introduction—in all of the guides because they bookend the highest purpose of our journey here: connecting to our goddess nature.

Since connection to ourselves is key, here are a few simple ways to reconnect to one's self.

Simple Heart Connectors

Place your hand over your heart. Listen for the heartbeat. Breathe. Take as long as you need to feel reconnected.

To me, it's a feeling of calm followed by the warmth of love radiating through the body. You'll feel what you feel.

You can also simply affirm to yourself: *I love and accept myself.* This affirmation is one of the most powerful ones I know, and repeating it like a mantra can change your whole energy. It's like giving yourself a hug and throwing yourself a private party for being you.

Another way of connecting to the heart involves folding your fingers into your palms and placing your knuckles together over your heart. This is called "Bear Pose," and it activates the heart chakra beautifully and connects the energies of the body.

If you have a lot of blocks in your body, it might take a while before you start to feel your own energy. I recommend working on transmuting and deleting the stories creating the blocks—like we've done around specific topics in these guides.

HUGGING IT OUT

Out of sync with a loved one? I recommend what I call "hugging it out."

One of my best friends taught this to me, and at first, I was so uncomfortable. He'd hold me for minutes. I was aware of his body and his breath. I thought, "When is he going to let me go?" But I knew he was expressing his love for me, and I didn't want to cut him off. I also knew I needed to work on the reasons for my discomfort.

I knew being held by someone I completely loved and trusted, who loved and trusted me, shouldn't cause me discomfort. My friend was teaching me how to receive love through a hug, and not just a little "I love you" hug, but a whole body, "I'm so glad you're in my life and love you to pieces" hug.

He was also getting us in sync with each other, and I discovered very quickly that a long hug like that between two willing parties (okay, I was determined too) creates a harmony in energies.

"Hugging it out" is also the perfect antidote

to those moments or days when we aren't feeling much love and joy whatsoever. Ask someone for a hug if you need it.

Around my house, we commonly ask someone who doesn't seem like themselves, "Do you need a hug?" It's our go-to and has transformed person-to-person interactions faster than anything I've ever seen.

Energy Booster & Grounder

Looking for more energy? Who doesn't want that? Putting your hand on the crown of your head works wonders. Depending on how tired you are, you might need to leave it there for a while or even tap it to break up some of the blockages there. The energies in the body rise up to meet your hand. That's why it works. Again, the power of touch, right?

Stomping your feet also works wonders. Again, the energy you generate by stomping your feet also stirs the energies.

And it helps ground you if you're feeling what some people call "spacey" or "flighty." It makes you feel your feet, something

I cultivate on a daily basis given how my energy works.

Prayer & Meditation

When people ask me what I've done to become such a joyful person (trust me, I haven't always been), I note how much meditation and prayer boost my life.

Ever since I could speak, I've prayed. But when I added meditation to it, my spiritual practice became even richer.

To me, meditation isn't just about clearing your mind of thoughts. It's about connecting to the love in your heart, which spreads out to your whole being. That's what calms the mind and body and connects us to the divine. We've talked about this a lot.

To me, the only difference between a "great" meditation and "great" sex is semantics. I get to the same place—either with a partner or on my own.

You might be saying, "Seriously, Ava?" Mediation is as great as sex? Yep.

But I know not everyone has discovered this yet. I've had so many people tell me they have trouble meditating. They don't feel they're doing it right.

Most of the people who've told me this have tried to use meditation solely to clear their minds. From their thoughts, in case you were wondering.

But when they started getting in touch with their hearts like I suggested—even by something as simple as listening to their heartbeat—they found it much easier to meditate and even more powerful. It's that heart chakra piece we've discussed before.

For me, connecting to my goddess nature and the Universe or the Divine or whatever you want to call it (basically LOVE) is the single most beautiful gift I've ever given myself. It keeps delivering an endless fountain of joy.

And I do meditate as a practice every day, even if it's only for a few minutes.

But I also know I am connected to my goddess nature and the Divine at all times now in a way I never used to be, so I dance with the practice differently than I did in the past.

Your spiritual practices will evolve as you evolve. The trick is to remain open and flexible and not become rigid in these things we term "practices." And if you find yourself developing stories and beliefs around them or anything else, it's time to bring out the Blaster, our reclaiming practice. Speaking of which...

RECLAIMING PRACTICES: DELETING THE STORIES

Have a thought or a story or belief you don't want to have? We've talked about this a lot in the guides, but let's review it here again.

Simply say, *I transmute and delete X.* As many times as you need to blast it out. Or you can use, *I forgive myself for believing X.*

Need to forgive someone and release yourself from negative interactions in your life?

Just repeat, *X, I release you from the role you are playing for me. Go in peace. All is forgiven and released.*

Feeling pissed off?

I surround my anger with light and love; all is forgiven and released.

Not sure what your stories are? Listen to yourself. Ask the Universe to show them to you. Maybe even ask a loving friend for his or her thoughts. Or work with a professional.

Your goddess nature will help guide you. Trust me. The stories will come up when you decide to take this journey of self-discovery and healing. Your goddess nature has mandated it.

Easy Calming Practice

Need help calming yourself down from anxiety, paranoia, or hysteria?

Try saying the sound "Heeee," either to yourself or out loud.

I've had friends do this, and they suddenly felt light-headed. Why? Because they were so amped up on anxiety and worry, the corresponding relief their system experienced was tremendous. Pent-up emotion sometimes does that on its way out. It's like we've turned our emotional faucet on high, and it's flooding out of us.

But trust me... This one is a winner. I used it on many scary nights in warzones when I'd jump at every sound or simply couldn't sleep because I was too anxious to rest.

FANNING

Huh? Yeah, you heard me. Get out a magazine or a piece of paper—or even a real Spanish lace ladies' fan. When you feel sluggish or crummy, fan yourself. Why? It breaks the heavy energy up in your energetic field. And it works... I taught this to my sister to help my niece when she was super little. She was picking up a lot of junk from other kids at daycare, and fanning brushed it off. Her mood immediately improved. She was happy again and back to herself. It's funny, but when she was three years old, she started picking up a magazine and fanning her mother when she had a "bad" day at the hospital. My niece knew what to do. She was still in touch with her goddess nature.

Native Americans and other cultures have been using this practice—likely under different names—for centuries. I can't recommend it enough.

Simple Chakra Openers

Curious about opening up your chakras more after all this talk about how it opens us up to more love and joy in the body?

Here are a couple of simple ways: color and sound. You can wear a color you feel drawn to or one you intuit you need to boost your energy.

And you can say the sound of that chakra out loud or to yourself. I loved seeing that "Yum," something I say all the time for good food, was the heart sound. Made sense to me. Food makes me happy.

Chakra	Color	Sound
Root	Red	Lum
Sacral	Orange	Vum

Solar Plexua	Yellow	Rum
Heart	Green to Pink	Yum
Throat	Turquoise	Hum
Third Eye	Indigo	Om
Crown	Purple to White	(Silent-no sound)

You can check out tons of other things about chakras online if you want. There is no limit to what you can learn.

Shifting Pain, Blockages & Other Physical Issues

The body is wired to communicate your emotional, mental and spiritual nature with you. Like the stars guiding a ship, the body is your guide in this journey called life. Here are some common areas of pain and blockage and their corresponding stories along with some helpful tidbits to shift them. Of course, if they are chronic, you will likely need to deal with both the physical aspects of the situation as well as the mind-body connection.

Personally, I've experienced a lot of illness and injury in my life. Sometimes I needed to use medicine and physical therapy as well as digging deeper into the root causes of the pain. When I cleared the cause, my body healed faster and completely.

Body Signal	Story	Shift
Back	Where don't you feel supported? By yourself or others?	Write them out and do the Reclaiming practice. And nurture yourself.
Shoulders	What burdens are you carrying around? Either for yourself or others?	Write them out and do the Reclaiming practice. And nurture yourself.
Neck	What thoughts are too big to realize? To heavy to carry right now?	Write them out and do the Reclaiming practice. And nurture yourself.

Knees	What childhood issues or patterns with your parents are still playing out?	Write them out and do the Reclaiming practice. And nurture yourself.
Yeast Infections	Where do you feel ashamed in your life and actions and with whom?	Write them out and do the Reclaiming practice. Say the word Lum (for the root chakra/genital area).
Head aches	What are you obsessing about, and where don't you feel the Divine listens or supports you?	Write them out and do the Reclaiming practice. Say the word Om or be silent.
Sore Throat	What aren't you expressing?	Write them out and do the Reclaiming practice. Say the word Hum. Draw or write something.

Heart Issues	Where do you feel not loved or incapable of love?	Write them out and do the Reclaiming practice. Say the word Ha (for the physical heart) and Yum.
Liver and Gall Bladder	Where are you frustrated, enraged, or overwhelmed?	Write them out and do the Reclaiming practice. Say the word Shoo and imagine green light surrounding the organs.
Lungs and Large Intestine	What is making you sad or what are you grieving over? What can't you let go of?	Write them out and do the Reclaiming practice. Say the word Zzzz, and imagine white light surrounding the organs.
Kidneys and Bladder	What are you afraid of? What can't you hold or carry anymore in your life?	Write them out and do the Reclaiming practice. Say the word Shwoo, and imagine turquoise light surrounding the organs.

Stomach, Spleen, Pancreas	Where don't you feel nurtured? Where can't you digest life?	Write them out and do the Reclaiming practice. Say the word Who and imagine yellow light surrounding the organs.
Hands	What are you afraid to reach for? What don't you feel you can grasp?	Write them out and do the Reclaiming practice. Link your hands in prayer-style and rotate them clockwise and counter-clockwise.
Feet	Where are you afraid to move forward? Where can't you reach?	Write them out and do the Reclaiming practice. Imagine yourself walking to the places that you're scared of, the ones you really want to go to. Believe you can do it!

Eyes	What are you afraid to see? Where can't you see the highest version of you and your life?	Write them out and do the Reclaiming practice. Repeat Om to clear your vision, and rub your hands together and lay the palms over your eyes, affirming you are willing to see.
Ears	What are you afraid to hear? What can't you hear to help you receive the guidance you need?	Write them out and do the Reclaiming practice. Rub your hands together and lay the palms over your ears, affirming you are willing to hear.

These are only meant to be landmark suggestions based on my experience and those I have known. Your goddess nature ultimately knows best. Listen to it. Just make sure you clear any blind spots to uncovering what's going on and what you need to do to clear it—for all time.

W̲ʀɪᴛɪɴɢ & J̲ᴏᴜʀɴᴀʟɪɴɢ

Expressing yourself in written form is a powerful way of connecting to your deepest thoughts and emotions. Many of us find the privacy of a journal or a tablet that is only for our eyes the one place we don't have to censor ourselves. If we're angry, we can write out all the reasons why (and there's sometimes great satisfaction if we decide to burn up or shred those reasons as a way of letting them go). If we're sad, we can express all the reasons, anything from, "No one loves me" to "My spouse no longer makes me happy."

We can write out a sex scene or fantasy as a way of getting in touch with what we want, something I can't recommend highly enough. (You might even consider sharing this with your partner.) You might describe your dream job or dream relationship.

The power of using words consciously can produce miracles. We can heal ourselves. We can illuminate our deepest wishes and desires. We can change how we approach whatever's bothering us. We can manifest something we truly want.

For a long time, I kept a gratitude journal in addition to writing about the various things that bothered me. Every night, I would write down at least three things I was grateful for that had happened that day. I began this practice when I was recovering from a difficult surgery and facing ongoing physical issues. With all of the pain, isolation (I couldn't walk), and physical therapy, it was sometimes a struggle to come up with three items for my journal.

But over the course of my own healing, it became much easier. I got excited when my daily gratitude list grew. Sometimes I could think of as many as ten or twenty things that had happened that day to rock my world. And so my world changed…

The other thing I did in my daily journal was write down all of the things I was doing to better love and heal myself. I even calculated the amount of time I was devoting to it on a daily basis. That changed things too. My life became richer because a part of me needed to see love and growth made tangible. When it was so much a part of me, I didn't need to catalogue it any more. It was just a part of my life. I gave myself what

I needed when I needed it.

Play with what you might need to write or journal about. Maybe it's even writing letters to people that you don't plan on sending. Whatever it is, expressing your thoughts and feelings makes you more present with yourself and your needs. The conversation you have with your goddess woman self will be a beautiful one.

Vision Boards

Just as our written words carry the power of intention, so too do the images with which we surround ourselves. Images can be used to portray something we want, something we believe we will manifest.

You can do a vision board on anything really. I've done ones about my career, my life, my wedding, my home, and even one chronicling pictures of myself at the various stages of my life. I'm an artist to the core, and I love taking an idea I have in my head and finding a picture that represents it.

I used to gather up old magazines from various places and go to town. I cut different sizes and shapes of cardboard, and I would arrange them like a collage. Once I did that, using a combination of words and images, I would place it in a spot in my house that I would see. A specific word or image would catch my eye, giving me a message of what I needed to remember or focus on.

Our higher selves and the Divine are always cheerleading us on, and they will use any available means to communicate with us and get our attention. Let's dive in a little deeper...

DIVINE SIGNS & SYMBOLS

The world is as mystical as we allow it to be, and for millennia, people have been paying attention to signs and symbols from the Divine and writing about them. The more I asked for guidance from the Universe, the more things started showing up in *my* universe. I'd see a billboard with a message on it or a catch-phrase in a TV commercial that raised the hairs on my arms.

Then I noticed a white owl on the fence across from my house during the day, something I'd never seen before. Many non-Christian religions have whole books on the symbolic meanings of animals and birds. For example, an owl signifies that you are in touch with your own wisdom— or that you need to be. You get the drift.

Keep an eye out for what's showing up for you. You might be surprised what it tells you or confirms.

Stones & Crystals

What about stones and crystals, you might ask? Really, are we going to go that woo-woo? Yes, because woo-woo is just another story.

I used to think they were just rocks, and that people who liked them were a little woo-woo. Do I love stones and crystals now? You bet.

I discovered their energy accidentally (at least unconsciously). I was in Egypt for business and spent a weekend I had off in Luxor, where I visited an alabaster factory. Two Egyptian men gave me two hunks of that beautiful stone. I was deeply moved, but when I was packing to go home, I thought, "These rocks weigh a ton and what am I going to do with them anyway?"

But I couldn't bring myself to throw them away.

Years later, I was sitting at my computer when I heard one of my guides tell me to pick up the alabaster (yes, I can hear my guides talking to me, although this has been an evolution). For those of you wondering what I'm talking about it, a guide is like your guardian angel or a spirit that's been assigned to help you on your journey, but back to the story...

I went ahead and picked the darn thing up, and wouldn't you know it? For the first time, I could feel energy in what I had thought was an inanimate object.

And it was powerful.

I was also told to look up the meaning of alabaster and discovered it aided in abating anger and encouraging forgiveness, two things I needed help with, especially at that time.

Until then, I didn't know that stones have

energies, and soon I discovered a whole slew of helpers. It blows my mind how much of nature's gifts are related to spiritual support.

My intuition knew what I needed. Yours will too if it's something your goddess nature has planned.

ASTROLOGY

Have you ever looked at your horoscope? Well, astrology has been a guiding force for people for millennia and is chock full of guiding principles and support. If it resonates with you, check it out.

I kinda didn't know what I was getting into when a healer suggested I contact her friend to have my birth chart read, but when I heeded her advice, my mind was blown. She'd given me a map of who I was as a goddess woman and the lessons my soul had arranged for me in this life. I was moved to tears when I finished listening.

The accuracy was mind-blowing, and all she'd had to go on was my birth date and time of my birth.

I like to think that the Divine arranged for us each to have our own private life map in the stars at the moment of our birth. Certainly in centuries past, this birth map was considered to be a powerful source of wisdom to guide one's life.

Yoga & Other Physical Practices

Yoga has become one of the most popular practices to connect the body with the spirit. The movements are designed to open up the body's energies, but other practices like Qi gong and tai chi do so as well.

Like everything else, when you add love and intention to anything, you take it to a higher level. I have always found that to be the case with these practices.

Energy Healing & Other Modalities

How about alternate energy modalities? I have found acupuncture to be wonderful, but once I discovered energy healing, it was like a super-charged rocket had blazed through my life.

I shifted easier and faster from old beliefs and cleared blockages in ways that served my highest good. I got down to the root causes instead of band-aiding issues or moving or clearing energy that showed up time and time again.

When my own healing gifts blew into my life, I found myself helping others in the same way. If you need it, I can't recommend it enough. Your goddess nature will lead you to the right people. I also note a few healers I have personally worked with on my website.

Trust Your Intuition

Looking for more tips? Pay attention to where your hand unconsciously rests on your body, or what your intuition is telling you to do.

Your goddess nature will always show you the way.

Enjoy the ride, goddess woman.

It truly is a wonderful life.

The Goddess Guides to Being a Woman

Goddesses Decide:

Relearning Divine Power

Stop buying all the lies that say you can't have the life you want. You're a goddess woman. Reclaim your true power.

Goddesses Deserve The Gs:

Linking Self-Worth with Material Abundance

Become the goddess moneymaker you were born to be. Believe you're worth all the abundance you set your sights on.

Goddesses Love Cock:

Re-establishing the Divine Connection

Get it on like a goddess! Bring joy and connection back into the bedroom.

Goddesses Cry and Say Motherfucker:
Erasing Shame from Human Expression
Forget all you've learned about getting angry or sad and everything in between... Express yourself like a goddess.

Goddesses Don't Do Drama:
Removing Toxicity from Relationships
Say no to toxic peeps and all their crap and start building the loving and joyful relationships you truly want.

Goddesses Are Sexy:
Enjoying a Loving Self-Image
Delete all the stories saying you aren't beautiful or sexy. Start believing it today!

Goddesses Eat:
Reclaiming a Divine Partnership with Food
Throw off all the soul-sucking stories about food. Learn to feast like a goddess woman.

Goddesses Are Happy:
Living a Fulfilling Life
Find your inner happy place as a goddess woman. Start enjoying life!

Goddesses Face Fear:
Tapping into Divine Courage
Face down your fears and demons like a goddess woman. Tap into your innate courage!

MORE GODDESS GUIDES ARE COMING...

Sign up for my newsletter www.avamiles.com to keep up-to-date for your next powerful goddess woman shift.

Goddess Memo from Ava

Hey Goddess Woman!

Thank you for sharing The Goddess Guides journey with me! It's a joy to be connected to a divine rockstar like you.

If you leave a review, I want to thank you up front. Every time a reader takes the time out of her busy schedule to share her feelings about my books, I'm so grateful.

And if you decide to tell friends or co-workers about The Goddess Guides because they just have to read them… Well, you've changed your world and helped more women become the goddess women they want to be. From one goddess woman to another, I want to bless you for it. And you will be. Trust me.

Until we meet again, have fun being your amazing goddess woman self.

Lots of love,

Ava

Author Bio

International bestselling author Ava Miles calls herself a divine rockstar—something she believes everyone is deep down. Ava spent many years traveling the world and sharing her gifts with women and men in war-torn countries, helping them to rebuild and reintegrate their communities amidst intense struggle. She has managed multi-million-dollar projects for international agencies, such as the United Nations.

Now, she brings that experience together with her passion for sparking joy and personal success in people's lives in *The Goddess Guides to Being A Woman*.

For more information about Ava, visit www.avamiles.com.